THE EDGE

How to Stand Out
by Showing You're All In
(For Emerging Leaders and Those Who Lead Them)

**ADAM TARNOW &
DAVID MORRISON**

HOUNDSTOOTH
PRESS

THE EDGE
How to Stand Out by Showing You're All In
(For Emerging Leaders and Those Who Lead Them)

FIRST EDITION

ISBN   978-1-5445-3523-4 *Hardcover*
       978-1-5445-3216-5 *Paperback*
       978-1-5445-3215-8 *Ebook*
       978-1-5445-3287-5 *Audiobook*

To our wives: you both make standing out look easy.
This book was written for everyone else.

CONTENTS

INTRODUCTION

THAT POKER SHOW ON ESPN

"You 'might' have this job. Let's see how it goes." That's basically what Dabo Swinney was being told by his organization's leadership. It was October 13, 2008, and this charismatic young man with a funny nickname[1] had just been named *interim* head coach of Clemson University's football team (the Clemson Tigers).

At the time of his promotion, the team was 3–3. Even though many college football programs would be content with this record, for Clemson, it was disappointing. Hopes were high in 2008. The team was preseason ranked No. 9 in the nation, and many believed this would be a breakout year for them. After six games, hope was lost, and head coach Tommy Bowden resigned a few days after a 12–7 loss to No. 24–ranked Wake Forest University.

---

[1] "Dabo" is what William Christopher's three-year-old brother called him after he was born. It's short for "that boy."

To a fractured team and a skeptical fan base, the decision to promote Dabo looked puzzling. This was understandable. The season started with conversations about a national championship. Now, in mid-October, everyone was simply hoping to make a post-season bowl game.

At the press conference announcing him as interim head coach, here's what Dabo had to say:

> My job is to try to lead these guys. Love these guys. To get them to love each other. To get them to play hard and believe in each other, and get back-to-back, and circle the wagons and believe in what we're doing. Believe that we can have a special season, and we still have an opportunity to do that.

> There's a lot of things still on the table for this football team. I can't sit here and tell you I can see the future. I have no idea. All I can tell you is the guys that run out there this Saturday and every Saturday for the next month and a half or two months, they're going to be playing with their hair on fire. That's the best we're going to do. We're going to unify this group, and we're going to play as one. One heartbeat. Everybody playing together.

> That's our only chance. As I told them, I gave every one of them the opportunity: "If you can't do this, this, this, and this, then you need to go get your stuff out of your locker and head on out of here and your scholarship is honored. But, if you show up on that practice field tonight, you better be *all in.*"

> My thing is our backs are against the wall. You ever watch that poker show on ESPN? I love that poker show. We got pocket tens,

we don't have a great hand, but we got a chance, so we're going *all in*. I need these players to be *all in*, and we'll see what happens.[2]

After that press conference, people were a tad less skeptical. However, that was just a press conference. The real question was whether the team would perform on the field.

Dabo had said he had two messages for his team. One, the team was going to be united. Two, everyone needed to play like they were *all in*. Five days later, even after a disappointing loss, it was clear the message was received *and* believed, and the rest of the season went well. The team won four of their last six games, they were invited to play in the Gator Bowl, and on December 1, 2008, Dabo had the "interim" title removed and was named the twenty-seventh head coach of the Clemson Tigers football team.

Since being named head coach, and at the time of this writing, Dabo's record is 150–36, and he's won seven ACC Championships, played in eleven bowl games, and won in two national championships (while appearing in four national championship games).[3] Clemson has gone from a perennial underperforming team to one of the best programs in the history of college football.

Over the span of Dabo's career, his message has remained the same: As a team, we're a family. As an individual, you must be

---

2   Dabo Swinney, "TigerNet.com–Dabo Swinney Coins the Phrase 'All In' in First Interim Head Coach Presser at Clemson," ClemsonTigerNet, November 16, 2014, YouTube video, https://www.youtube.com/watch?v=1ATKf5wQo_Q.

3   Wikipedia, s.v. "Dabo Swinney," last modified June 5, 2022, 18:08, https://en.wikipedia.org/wiki/Dabo_Swinney.

all in. "When you're *all in*, you are committed to doing the best you can in everything that you do. Being a person of excellence."[4]

The team adopted and still uses a pregame ritual that allows each member of the team to communicate they are *all in*. Prior to every game, poker chips are placed in a player's locker. When the team leaves the locker room, a member of the coaching staff is standing at the door with an *all in* bucket. No player can leave the locker room and take the field until they place all their chips into the bucket to symbolize that they are *all in*.

Dabo and the coaching staff know exactly what they want. As they recruit new players, they are looking for talent *and* an *all in* attitude. As they develop their current players, the coaching staff is focused on skill development *and* attitude development. It's not enough to be a talented football player. Dabo has figured out that world-class talent alone doesn't win championships, unify a team, or build a culture of excellence. Winning, unity, and culture are created with *heart*. Talent is expected, but that doesn't always differentiate players. At Clemson, attitude, character, and mindset—those are what separate a good player from a great player.

I THOUGHT THIS BOOK WAS SUPPOSED TO HELP MY CAREER?

What on earth does this story about a college football coach have to do with you and your career? Over the years, we've noticed something. What's true at Clemson is true at most organizations. Most team leaders are looking for the exact same thing as the Clemson coaching staff. Most team leaders want more than

---

4   Dabo Swinney, "Dabo Swinney on Being the Best YOU," Coach Schuman's NUC Sports Football Channel, May 10, 2019, YouTube video, https://www.youtube.com/watch?v=EGKKha2ktCU.

talent. Why do they want more? Because talent is a commodity. Talented people are a dime a dozen. The current workforce here in the United States is as educated and talented as ever. Organizations aren't struggling to find the right talent. They are struggling to find the right combination of talent *and* attitude.

Your résumé is no longer what sets you apart. Even if you are a self-motivated, detail-oriented team player who can think outside the box. The path to standing out, getting ahead, and making an impact requires more than a degree, a certification, or great work experience. Talent, smarts, and experience are no longer your competitive advantage.

EMOTIONAL COMMITMENT IS YOUR NEW ADVANTAGE

When team leaders hear about the culture at Clemson, they are jealous. Why? Because they want what Clemson's got. They want to lead organizations and teams full of people who want to work hard, pursue excellence, and bring their best, every day. They want everyone to be *all in*. Organizational psychologists call this "employee engagement."

Employee engagement is and has been a popular topic in corporate America for the past ten years. It's defined as "the emotional commitment the employee has to the organization and its goals."[5]

The key phrase there is "emotional commitment." Employee engagement doesn't measure an employee's happiness or satisfaction. It's about an employee's emotional commitment to the

---

5   Kevin Kruse, "What is Employee Engagement," *Forbes*, June 22, 2012, https://www.forbes.com/ sites/kevinkruse/2012/06/22/employee-engagement-what-and-why/?sh=647eadd97f37.

team or organization. It's an objective way to tell if someone is *all in*.

We know we've never met your boss or your team leader, but we know what they want. They want talent *and* emotional commitment. They want a team filled with people whose attitude and character instill confidence and trust.

Your boss wants you (and everyone else in the organization) to be *all in*. This attitude is what separates good employees from great employees. This attitude is what gives your career an EDGE (more on that later). This *all in* attitude is what causes you to stand out.

THERE'S NEVER BEEN A BETTER TIME TO BE *ALL IN*

In some ways, we wish we could start our careers over right now. Why? Emotional commitment is low. There has never been a better time to be an emerging and engaged leader than right now.

The large number of disengaged employees and the game-changing impact of *all in* players are why you, regardless of how early you are in your career, have such a great opportunity. There has never been a better time to stand out, get noticed, and make an impact.

Combined, we have over forty years of work experience. We've worked part-time jobs, retail jobs, corporate jobs, and nonprofit jobs. We've worked for big organizations and small organizations, and we have seen one thing time and again: all bosses want to lead a team filled with people who are emotionally committed. People who are *all in.*

So how do you show you're *all in*? How can you live this out practically? We will show you four simple yet profound ways to let the people around you know you are emotionally committed. The good news is you can start to implement these behaviors right away, and by implementing these behaviors you won't have to suck up, sell out, or double-cross anyone. You can be you.

The behaviors we're going to share with you have a tremendous amount of flexibility regarding implementation. Our list is not a prescription, but rather a description, and you can tailor it to fit you and your situation.

Here is what will give you the EDGE:

Energy—the positive attitude you bring every day.

Diligence—the way you approach your work with care and persistence.

Growth—the hunger for progress and development you embody.

Endurance—the character you demonstrate in the face of difficulty.

This book will serve as a playbook of sorts. It will give you the motivation and ideas you need to begin taking control of your career and start making an impact. These four items will prepare you for your next promotion and make you indispensable to your organization. This is not only what your boss is looking for but also what will make you a leader worth following.

So with that being said, let's drop our poker chips into the bucket and get moving. It's time to start showing you're *all in*.

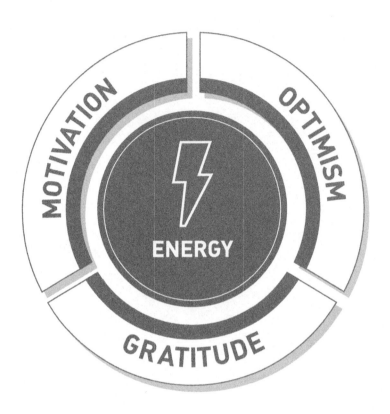

PART 1

ENERGY

THE POSITIVE ATTITUDE *YOU* BRING EVERY DAY

CHAPTER 1

MOTIVATION

THE TED TALK THAT SHOOK THE WORLD

Maybe we're being a little dramatic. It didn't shake the world, but it sure made an impact.

Simon Sinek's talk "Start With Why: How Great Leaders Inspire Action" went viral and became the latest way to sound smart around other people. Sinek's talk asserted that great leaders and organizations focus on *why* they do what they do instead of *what* they do and *how* they do it.

At the bar: "You know, I'm really in a season right now where I'm trying to determine my *why*. If I can unlock that, I know I'll have a successful and rewarding career. I know that sounds deep, but I really feel strongly that I need to make this connection between my *career* and my *why*."

In a team meeting: "Honestly, I think the problem with your growth plan is that we haven't told our customers *why* we exist. People care about *why* we exist. We don't exist just to make glowin-the-dark dog toys. There's a bigger reason for our existence, and we need to make that clear. If we do that, we can become the Apple of dog toys."

For years, it was all anyone seemed to talk about. Keynote messages, blog posts, *Fast Company* articles, leadership books, podcasts—everyone was referencing Mr. Sinek's *start with why* principle.

I thought it would be a phase. I thought sooner or later, everyone would get over it and laugh about our brief obsession with *why*.

Here I am over a decade later, and that day hasn't come. Why? (No pun intended.) Because this principle is so helpful and applicable to so many different areas of life.

THE PRINCIPLE AND YOUR CAREER

If you haven't watched the TED Talk or read Sinek's book, the message can be summarized with five bullet points:

1. Your *why* is your purpose, cause, or belief.

2. Every inspiring leader and organization, regardless of size or industry, starts with *why*.

3. People don't buy *what* you do; they buy *why* you do it.

4. Knowing our *why* is essential for lasting success and to avoid being lumped in with others.

5. When your *why* goes fuzzy, it becomes much more difficult

to maintain the growth, loyalty, and inspiration that helped drive your original success.[6]

I know you probably already see the connection between Sinek's principle and your career, but I'll say it anyway. What's true for organizations is true for you. If you understand your *why*, your career will be more sustainable, more fulfilling, and more successful.

However, this is where I'm going to say goodbye to Mr. Sinek and 2009. I'm not going to tell you to camp at your local coffee shop and journal until you discover your *why*. I'm not going to give you a series of exercises that makes finding your *why* easy.

Why? (Again, no pun intended.) Because finding your *why* is not easy! You can't figure out your purpose, cause, or belief in a few hours, scribbling in a journal. This is not the way real life works.

In my experience, discovering your personal *why* is a journey. Of course, there will be exceptions to this rule, but generally speaking, I've never met anyone who figured out their *why* through anything other than experience.

WHY LEADS TO MOTIVATION; MOTIVATION LEADS TO ENERGY

When you know your *why*, you tap into something powerful as it relates to your career: motivation. I've never met a motivated person who wasn't also energetic. If you are not motivated to do what you do, it will be very difficult to consistently bring the energy of a positive attitude.

---

6   Sam Thomas Davies, "*Start with Why* by Simon Sinek," *Sam T. Davies* (blog), accessed June 17, 2022, https://www.samuelthomasdavies.com/book-summaries/business/start-with-why/.

If you want to stand out by showing you're *all in*, then you need to first and foremost know and understand what motivates you—in other words, your *why*.

CHANCES ARE, YOU'VE ALREADY TRIED TO FIND YOUR WHY

Most people choose a career based on their interests and motivation. For example, I chose to study accounting in college. Did I do this because my dad and grandfather were both accountants? It's true, they were, but that's not why. Did I do this because I was born on April 16 (the day after Tax Day)? Again, this is true, but no. Did I do this because I wanted to endure a life of jokes about pocket protectors and assumptions that I'm socially awkward? No! (And, sadly, also true.)

I chose that career path because, for some reason, it was my favorite class in high school, and I was motivated to learn more about the subject. I followed my *motivation*, which provided me with *energy* and kept me *focused*.

Motivation is essential to a fulfilling career. This is both good news and bad news. The good news: it's possible for everyone to have a satisfying career. The bad news: you have to figure out what motivates you.

Again, in my experience, I haven't met many emerging leaders who are able to clearly articulate what motivates them. This lack of clarity causes all kinds of issues. The primary issue is you end up choosing a career path for unsustainable reasons.

Money, title, cool office space, a short commute. These may seem like great reasons to take a job or choose a career; however, the luster will fade. There are greater factors that will lead to more sustainable motivation. To that end, here are three ideas we think will help you on your motivation journey—three ideas that might help you begin to discover your *why*.

Idea #1: Study the Puzzle Pieces

We like to think finding your motivation is like putting together a jigsaw puzzle, but with a twist. Unlike a normal jigsaw puzzle where every piece in the box fits together, the motivation puzzle is one that comes with one hundred pieces, but only a few pieces need to combine to complete the puzzle. The other pieces look like they might fit, but they don't. That's the twist.

Figuring out your *why*—what motivates you—is the strangest puzzle you'll ever solve. The hard work isn't so much finding your *few* pieces. The hard work is eliminating all the pieces that *don't* fit. Most people don't get through the sorting process. They give up and just float through life and hop around from one unfulfilling job to another.

As you attempt to put together your puzzle of motivation, consider some of the most common pieces, many of which are likely to *fit* you.[7]

---

7   These puzzle pieces are inspired by two valuable resources on this topic: Daniel Pink's book *Drive: The Surprising Truth About What Motivates Us* (New York City: Riverhead Books, 2009) and Patrick Lencioni's book *The Truth About Employee Engagement: A Fable About Addressing the Three Root Causes of Job Misery* (Hoboken, NJ: Jossey-Bass, 2015).

PUZZLE PIECE	DESCRIPTION
Autonomy	You feel like you have some influence over the *how* and *what* of accomplishing a task or goal.
Mastery	You feel like you are growing and developing in skillfulness.
Impact	You know your job is making someone's life better.
Connection	You feel known and appreciated by your boss and peers.
Purpose	You feel like your job is making the world a better place.
Results	You know how to define a win for your job and you feel like you are winning consistently.

What are you supposed to do with all of those words? As a simple guide, ask yourself these questions:

1. Which puzzle pieces best describe me?

2. Which puzzle pieces feel like they are missing from my career?

3. Which puzzle pieces de-motivate me?

4. Which puzzle pieces would my current team leader say motivate me the most?

5. What do I believe are my top two motivators?

These are not easy questions to answer, but taking some time to think through the motivators listed above is helpful as you ponder your *why*.

The list above can be helpful, especially if you are struggling to find motivation with your current job. Everyone goes through what our friend Chris Shelton calls "a work valley" from time to time. But if the valley persists for more than a few months, it might point to a lack of motivation. This doesn't mean all is lost. It might simply mean you need to have a conversation with your team leader or request a few tweaks to your job description. It's much easier to make changes to your current job than it is to find a new one.

Remember, the difficult part isn't finding the few pieces of your motivation puzzle—the difficult part is eliminating the other pieces. The more clarity you have on what motivates you, the easier it will be to find and select jobs that keep you engaged.

Idea #2: Don't Chase Money, Chase Match Quality

We know what you might be thinking after Idea #1. "Money. Money is what motivates me. If I got paid more money, then I'd be more engaged. If I made more money, I'd have no trouble showing I'm *all in*. I know money doesn't buy happiness, but money can buy a Vespa, and I've never seen an unhappy person on a Vespa."

We get it, and we'd like to offer a counterargument.

Many experts say that money is not a great motivator. Why? Because motivation is less about your *asset* list and more about your *to-do* list. In the end, you are always going to struggle with motivation if you do not like the actual work you are paid to do. If your task list doesn't match your strengths, passions, interests, gifts, and skills, you will still struggle when it comes to motivation.

Those who climb the new corporate ladder the fastest are those who have chosen careers with a high degree of match quality. I was introduced to the term "match quality" in David Epstein's book *Range*. Match quality refers to the fit between *what* you do and *who* you are.[8]

When it comes to your career, if you are consistently asking yourself how much money you can make in your profession, you will almost always find yourself struggling to show you're *all in*.

A better question to ask is, *Does this job match my skills and interests?* This question more often leads you to a motivating career. The more motivated you are, the more energy you have. The more energy you have, the more you stand out by showing you're *all in*.

Don't obsess about the money; obsess about the match quality.

Although finding a career that matches your skills and interests can be done at any stage, you'll waste a lot less time if you sort it out in your twenties. It's the life stage we affectionately call the "decade of getting your teeth kicked in." We know that sounds harsh, but it's an important step in career maturity.

It's during your twenties that you realize your parents, teachers, and coaches kind of lied to you—you can't be "anything you want to be." It's during your twenties that you realize you need to be what you were *created* to be. You were born with a certain set of gifts, interests, and personality traits. These gifts, interests, and traits need to match your career path. If they don't, you'll

---

8   David Epstein, *Range: Why Generalists Triumph in a Specialized World* (New York City: Riverhead Books, 2019).

have poor match quality. It doesn't matter how many Vespas you own. If there is poor match quality, you'll always struggle with motivation.

Your twenties are all about searching for match quality. Don't worry about what you studied in college. The cruelest part of college is how they make you pick a major when you're nineteen years old. Really? One thing is true about all nineteen-year-olds: they are at the peak of confidence but the valley of wisdom. Nineteen is not the best time to make a serious decision like *what should I do with the rest of my life.*

Your twenties are the new college years. Your twenties are a time to explore and run some match quality experiments.

If you have a good idea of what type of career matches your gifts, interests, and traits by the end of your twenties, then you are doing well! Your thirties will then become a decade of skill and experience accumulation.

It is during your thirties when you realize that, although you can't be "whatever you want to be," there are a few things you'll be great at doing. Your thirties can be an exciting time and a decade that gets you ready for your forties and fifties. For most professionals, their forties and fifties are when they kick ass and take names.

Of course, there are exceptions. For some people, it happens sooner (hello, LeBron). For some, it happens later (hello, your authors). If you are reading this and about to throw the book across the room because you are in your forties or fifties, we want to remind you of a Chinese proverb. "The best time to plant a tree was twenty years ago. The second-best time is now." It's never too late to act.

Regardless of what life stage you're in, the bottom line is this: don't chase money. Chase strong match quality. The money will always work itself out. Remember, it's about your to-do list, not a growing asset list.

Idea #3: What's Happening Today Is Getting You Ready for Tomorrow

If you genuinely desire to solve your puzzle of motivation and look for high match quality, then not only are you well on your way to finding a motivating career, but as a bonus, the risk of you wasting your life is low. How's that for a sweet little add-on?

Here's why we say that. If you are intentionally looking for how you will best serve the world with your skills and interests, that means every step of the journey is shaping who you are and who you are becoming.

There are plenty of ways to waste your life (we'll discuss one of them here in a moment). However, we have found those who earnestly seek to clarify their motivation and find a career with high match quality don't waste their life. Every step has a purpose.

If you go through a season in a bad job with a bad boss or you get fired for underperforming, those aren't failures; they're learning experiences that have helped you eliminate a few puzzle pieces.

If you intend to learn and look for the best match quality possible, then wasting time is almost impossible because everything you experience is helping to form who you are becoming. Sometimes, the best thing you can experience is something *not* going well.

The belief used to be that you need to pick a career path and never deviate from it, but many are realizing that trying on different jobs and careers isn't always the sign of a character defect (despite what the typical baby boomer will tell you). If you know a job or a career is not a fit for you, the faster you move on from that, the better.

The older we get, the more we realize life is like a *Seinfeld* episode. The genius of *Seinfeld* was that the writers could take what seemed like multiple completely different plot lines and perfectly bring them together at the end of each episode.

The most classic example must be episode fourteen of season five, titled "The Marine Biologist." As this episode progresses, two seemingly random plot lines transpire. Kramer decides to hit 600 Titleist golf balls into the ocean, and George is on a date with a woman who believes he's a marine biologist (because Jerry lied to her).

At the end of the episode, George tells Jerry and Kramer a story about something that happened while he and this woman took a romantic walk on the beach. There was a beached whale in distress. George's date, believing him to be a marine biologist, looked at him, expecting him to do something. George, not wanting to reveal the lie, approached the whale. In a brilliant monologue, George describes realizing that something was obstructing the whale's breathing and, after being tossed by a tidal wave, seeing something in the blowhole, reaching in, and pulling out...a Titleist.

What made that story so brilliant was no one saw it coming. No one could see how Kramer hitting golf balls into the ocean and Jerry lying to a woman about George being a marine biologist were going to come together. But when they did, it was pure gold.

This is how most careers end up. What seems random and disconnected suddenly connects and makes something that works. The dots never connect looking forward, only when looking back.

THANKS FOR THE WORDS, BUT I'M STILL NOT MOTIVATED

If none of these ideas changed the way you feel about your current situation, that's okay. You have at least three options:

1. **Be patient.** Do some personal puzzle-solving and see how you feel in three months. As we said, everyone goes through "work valleys." At the risk of sounding like one (or both) of your parents, we have to remind you that there's a reason work isn't called "recess." Sometimes it's hard, un-fun, demanding, and soul-crushing. We've all been there, and sometimes the best thing to do is just wait it out.

2. **Ask about changes to your current job description.** Consider sharing your insights from this chapter with your team leader and asking (not demanding) to change your job responsibilities. Come in with a plan—a list of responsibilities you're successfully managing, others you'd like to take on, and tasks you'd like to eliminate. The worst your

boss can say is no, and you shouldn't assume that will be the case. You'd be amazed at what people will agree to do when asked. Don't be afraid; make the request.

3. **Quit.** If you know that you're not a good fit for your current role, it's not just a work valley, and your team leader is unwilling to make changes to your job responsibilities, then it might be time to move on. It's rarely an easy decision, but neither is staying in a job that you're certain will never be a fit.

What do all three of these options have in common? They all require action. Doing nothing and hoping things get better is not an option. In fact, passively waiting for things to get better is a fast track to wasting your life. The lessons you learn from bad bosses, bad jobs, and even failure are all part of the puzzle-solving journey. But if you don't act upon what you are learning, that's a waste.

BOTTOM LINE: START RUNNING SOME MOTIVATION EXPERIMENTS

We've established that motivation is a strange puzzle, and the best way to solve that puzzle is to work at it. Try different tasks, explore different opportunities, and take good notes. No one is going to put their hand on your shoulder and say, "I know what you must be when you grow up." That kind of stuff literally only happens in movies and books. The rest of us must work hard to find our *why*.

The early part of your career is a great time to run some motivation experiments. Motivation experiments do two things. One, they help you find the pieces that fit your motivation puzzle, and two, they help you determine which pieces *do not* fit your motivation puzzle. I'll say it again: oftentimes it's more challenging to determine what pieces *don't* fit, rather than the pieces that *do* fit.

When it comes to running motivation experiments, draw inspiration from Thomas Edison, the famous American inventor. By the time he died in 1931, Thomas Edison had amassed close to 1,100 patents.[9] He held patents for electric light and power, the phonograph (the early form of the turntable record player), batteries, and the telephone. Thomas was motivated to invent, and he was clearly productive.

What we often don't remember about Thomas's story is how often he failed. He didn't only work on 1,100 inventions. He worked on many more. We don't know about these other inventions because they failed.

Along the way, Thomas developed a perspective on failure that motivated him to keep experimenting, evidenced by his famous quote: "I have not failed. I've just found 10,000 ways that won't work."

As you run your motivation experiments, don't worry if they fail. We'll talk about failure more in Chapter 10 (Resilience), but for now, know this: every failure gets you closer to solving your puzzle. There is not one universal map to success. Success is always idiosyncratic. It's always individual. But once you

---

9   History.com eds., "Thomas Edison," History.com, last modified June 6, 2019, https://www. history.com/topics/inventions/thomas-edison#:~:text=Thomas%20Alva%20Edison%20 was%20born,1847%2C%20in%20Milan%2C%20Ohio.&text=By%20the%20time%20he%20 died,and%2034%20for%20the%20telephone.

begin to figure out what keeps you motivated, special things can happen. That's when you'll do the best work, produce the best results, and find yourself climbing the new corporate ladder at a fast rate. That's the power of finding your *why*.

I'm sure you've already figured this out, but team leaders aren't huge fans of delivering pep talks every day. One of the most important jobs you have early in your career is to find your inner motivation. When you know *why* you do what you do, you will have a natural energy each day. When you know your *why*, showing that you're *all in* will rarely be an issue.

CHAPTER 2

OPTIMISM

BE YOUR SUPERHERO SELF

Be Yourself. Unless You Can Be Batman. Then Be Batman.

I saw that on a poster online and immediately wanted to buy it. When I saw it, my two sons were at the peak of their superhero phase. Of course, Batman was their favorite. He was (and still is) my favorite superhero too.

The poster made me laugh,[10] but it also contains a great message. The poster has three phrases. Let's break it down:

1. *Be Yourself.* That's a classic, no need to explain this one too much. As Oscar Wilde, the Irish poet and playwright, said so well, "Be yourself; everyone else is already taken." Your team doesn't need *fake you*, it needs *real you*.

2. *Unless You Can Be Batman.* Why would the poster say this?

---

10   The internet's good at that. Don't believe me? Just Google "Boaty McBoatface." You're welcome.

It is difficult to admit this, but some people don't know the details of Batman's life. Batman is a superhero, but his claim to fame is his *lack* of superpowers. Most of the other super-heroes have some form of a superpower. Wonder Woman has her bracelets. Superman has his super-strength. Aquaman has the ability to do the butterfly stroke. (Okay, we made up that last one, but seriously, who, besides Michael Phelps, knows how to do that stroke?) Batman, however, was just a regular, run-of-the-mill billionaire named Bruce Wayne. However, Bruce wanted to do something good for the world. He wanted to add value to his hometown. So rather than just sit around and hope someone else would handle the criminals, he decided to step up and fight crime. Bruce selflessly took initiative to make his world better. That's what made him a superhero. All kidding aside, that's a thoughtful lesson.

3. *Then Be Batman.* Given the choice between being our normal self or our selfless self, we are encouraged to be our selfless selves.

As we said, this poster has a pretty good message. Yes, be you because everyone else is already taken. However, recognize that while "being you," there is going to be a temptation to be a little lazy or a tad selfish. When you actively fight your inherent laziness and selfishness and try to do some good in the world, you become a superhero. You stand out. You get noticed.

A great way to become a superhero on your team is to choose positivity and optimism. For most people, this choice is not natural, especially in this post-COVID world. If you can fight against the negativity and pessimism that seems to be so prevalent in most people's lives, you'll get noticed.

OR BE A RAINBOW-PUKING UNICORN

If we were to include a free poster with this book, it would read: *Be Yourself. Unless You Can Be a Rainbow-Puking Unicorn. Then Be a Rainbow-Puking Unicorn.*

Said another way: *Be Yourself. Unless You Can Be Optimistic. Then Be Optimistic.*

Where did all of this talk about unicorns come from? Let us explain.

A friend, Clay Scroggins, wrote a fantastic book in 2017 titled *How to Lead When You're Not in Charge.* He highlighted four ways to lead from a position of *influence*, regardless of your title or rank in an organization. Clay asserted that if you (1) lead yourself, (2) choose positivity, (3) think critically, and (4) reject passivity, you will become a person of influence in your organization, regardless of where you sit within the organization.

That second one (positivity) can be especially challenging for some, and the pushback people give when they are encouraged to be optimistic can take many forms:

"What? You just want me to fake it?"

"Seriously, how can I *act* positive and optimistic when I don't *feel* positive or optimistic?"

"Okay. So, you just want me to walk around like a rainbow-puking unicorn? Great, I'll add that to my to-do list."

We get it. Who wants to be accused of being a rainbow-puking unicorn? No one, that's who.

Everyone is a little leery of the person who is optimistic 24/7. They are fun to watch on TV (think Ted Lasso, *30 Rock*'s Kenneth Parcell, or any character from a Disney Channel sitcom), but in real life, they don't necessarily instill trust.

When we meet optimistic people, we're skeptical.

"Why are you so happy?"

"What do you know that I don't know?"

"Why do you walk around whistling? That's weird."

This is why we appreciate Clay's insight. He reminds us that positivity is a choice. And choosing positivity doesn't mean you are giving up the ability to be authentic and believable. That is a helpful distinction.

WE COULD ALL USE A LITTLE OPTIMISM 'ROUND HERE

In the years since Clay released *How to Lead When You're Not in Charge*, we've learned a few things about the power of optimism. Optimism is an important aspect of leadership. If a leader doesn't believe tomorrow is going to be brighter than today, it will be difficult to follow that leader.

"I think tomorrow is going to be terrible and full of doom and gloom. Follow me there! I know the way!" said no leader ever (nor should they).

In the past five years, the world has experienced so many challenges. Natural disasters, social unrest, and a global pandemic. Not to sound too much like the end of an aforementioned Disney sitcom episode, but the world could benefit from a little more positivity and optimism. What is true in the world is true at your work too.

An optimistic attitude is an easy way to show you are *all in.* Optimism brings positive energy to your team. When you bring energy, you stand out.

If you can pull off being a rainbow-puking unicorn, then go for it. However, for the remaining 99.9 percent of you who don't feel like puking, we want to share three ideas we believe will help you choose positivity and optimism, regardless of the circumstances.

IDEA #1: LEARN TO BE A GOOD IMPROV PARTNER

Improv is a form of live theater in which the actors create the plot, characters, and dialogue of a game, scene, or story in the moment. *Whose Line Is It Anyway?* and most of the scenes from any Will Farrell movie are great examples of improv.

Although the actors are making things up on the spot, they are actually following a set of rules. For example, a general rule in improv is "yes, and," where the performer responds to whatever is said with "yes, and," then continues with a new statement. It perpetuates the energy and allows freedom. Other rules of improv are to simply say yes, to make statements, and to remember that there are no mistakes.

Experts in improv know that unhindered movement produces

energy. Unhindered movement is like rolling a big rock down a steep hill with nothing to block it. It keeps getting faster and faster the longer it rolls. That speed produces energy.

During improv, actors try to never say no. The word "no" hinders movement and energy. When partners say "yes" or "yes, and," the scene continues like a rock rolling down a big hill. It can't help but produce positive energy.

If you want to build the skill of positivity and optimism, start by practicing the rules of improv when you are with your team.

For example, let's say you are meeting with your team to talk about a new service offering in response to the pandemic.

Team Leader: *We need to pivot and begin offering our training classes online.*

Let's say you hear this, and some issues immediately come to mind. You know your team doesn't have the equipment to pull off this pivot, and you also don't have the cash flow to buy this new equipment. These two issues are facts. They are true. They warrant discussion.

Now you have a decision to make. Will you be an energy drain or an energy gain?

Energy drain: *But we don't own a camera or a quality microphone. And how are we going to pay for this gear? Canceling the last three live classes had a significant impact on our cash flow. Where are we going to get this cash? Do you think this is a good option for us right now?*

Energy gain: *Yes! That's a very creative idea* and *could help us weather the storm of this pandemic, and I'm sure we can brainstorm a creative way to find the cash flow to purchase the gear necessary to pull off this new venture.*

Notice something. In both of those responses, you made your point. You mentioned two facts that you believed were very important: a lack of cash and a lack of gear.

The difference, however, was *how* you responded. As an energy drain, you started with the word "but," and you questioned the idea. As an energy gain, you started with the word "yes." There is power in yes. Use that power to your advantage.

Choosing to be an energy gain builds agreement, camaraderie, and creative energy. Choosing to be an energy drain by asking hard-to-answer probing questions grinds the conversation to a halt.

Of course, I need to mention one qualifier. If your boss or team is discussing something illegal, discriminating, unjust, or untruthful, then don't say "yes, and." That's not good leadership. That's a great way to get you into a room where not much good happens: prison. If you don't believe me, just ask some ex-Enron employees. They'll tell you they wish they would have broken the rules of improv.

However, most organizations are trying to avoid illegal, discriminating, unjust, or untruthful activities. So for most of you reading this book, the rules of improv will help you bring energy to your team.

IDEA #2: FOCUS ON WHAT PEOPLE SEE, NOT JUST WHAT THEY HEAR

If security cameras recorded your movements at work with no sound, what would they record?

What does your body language communicate? What do your facial expressions communicate? What do your interactions with others and with your team communicate? I ask these questions because energy and positivity are often *seen* and not *heard*.

Next time you sit in a team meeting or on a virtual call, take a look around at your teammates. Do they "look" engaged? Who "looks" like they are emotionally committed, ready to work, and full of optimism and energy?

The way you carry yourself in a meeting is a simple way to bring energy. I know that sounds simple and trite, but it's true. Many times, that might be the only interaction you have with your team leader for a day or two.

Are you sitting up straight? Are you contributing to the conversation? Are you taking notes? Are you friendly with the other team members? Do you encourage people?

Or...

Are you slouching? Are you not saying anything? Are you checking your email? Are you largely ignoring your teammates? Are you rolling your eyes? Do you look like you'd rather be somewhere else?

I know, I know. It's not always fair to judge a book by its cover. I get it, and you're right. It's not fair.

But the cover design of the book still matters. Publishers don't ignore the design.

What you are feeling on the inside *always* shows on the outside. However, the reverse can also be true. What you project on the outside can impact the way you feel on the inside.

This idea of choosing to project something that is incongruent with what you are feeling inside is common to the human experience. Chances are, you're already an expert.

Who hasn't been in a terrible mood, and then the phone rings, and you answer as pleasantly as a Ritz-Carlton employee?

Or who hasn't been driving to a friend's house for dinner and fighting with your spouse during the entire commute, and then, as soon as your friend opens the door, your behavior changes: "Heeeeyyyyy! How are you?! We are sooooo excited to be here!"

Or you're sleeping in one morning, and a phone call wakes you up. You don't want to let the person on the other side of the line know you've been sleeping, so you force a burst of energy and answer the phone like you've been up for hours working out, eating bran muffins, and whistling.

The point I'm trying to make is this: you have some control over your energy levels.

When I encourage you to bring energy, I am not suggesting you change your temperament or core personality. I'm not suggesting that you "fake it till you make it." I'm not suggesting that you lie.

I am merely suggesting that you grow in your awareness of what kind of attitude you project and work hard to project an attitude of positivity.

You may not know this, but we have a podcast called *The Tacala Leadership Podcast*. You can't find it on Apple or Spotify. It's a private podcast for the team members at Tacala Companies (David's employer).

One of the most memorable and inspiring interviews we ever conducted on this podcast was with a young man named Timothy Alexander.

Timothy was a superstar high school athlete on his way to play Division One college football on a full scholarship. One summer before the start of college, Timothy was in a tragic car accident. This accident left him paralyzed. He was told he would never feel again or never eat alone, and he had no hope of any sense of a normal life.

Like something out of a movie, Timothy overcame all the odds. Yes, he is still paralyzed from the waist down and uses a wheelchair, but he can feed himself, can manage many tasks independently, and is living a fuller life than most people who can feel and walk.

Timothy is famous for the phrase, "It is what it is, but it's about what you make it." That is one of the most mature and realistic views of life I've heard in a long time.

"It is what it is..." Life is hard. Things happen. Stuff goes wrong.

"But it's about what you make it." You are not helpless. You are not out of control. An unfortunate circumstance may have come your way, but you do get to choose how you will respond.

Timothy is one of the most positive and optimistic people we've ever met, and he is a popular invitee because his energetic attitude is a breath of fresh air. We highly recommend his book *Ever Faithful, Ever Loyal: The Timothy Alexander Story*.

As an emerging leader, now is the time to practice bringing positivity and energy into everything you do.

Positivity keeps things moving forward.

Optimism is easier to work with than pessimism.

Energy is contagious and unifying.

IDEA #3: MANAGE YOUR FUEL

Anything that moves needs fuel. Including you. You cannot wait for someone to change your circumstances so your energy levels improve. You've got to manage your own fuel.

There is a dirty little secret of leadership that not many people discuss. Mentors and coaches are great and can prove to be very helpful as your career progresses. But no mentor or coach can lead you where you are *not willing* to lead yourself.

What you do when no one is looking will profoundly impact how you act when people are looking.

Again, here is something you already know, but we want to mention it anyway. Do you want to improve your energy levels? Then do these things:

1. Eat healthy food.

2. Exercise regularly.

3. Go outside often.

4. Get seven to eight hours of sleep every night.

5. Turn off social media.

6. Volunteer.

7. Generously support causes and charities you believe in.

8. Read books.

9. Listen to podcasts.

10. Take vitamins.

11. Talk to people face-to-face or on the phone.

12. Practice the discipline of journaling.

13. Turn off the radio in the car.

14. Write thank-you notes.

15. Encourage at least one person every day.

16. Build something with your hands.

17. Read a real newspaper.

18. Stop watching the news.

19. Get a pet.

20. Make your bed.

Who will force you to do any of the items on that list? Unless you are still living at home with your mom, no one.

The chances are high that nothing on the list above surprised you. You know what you need to do. Bringing energy is not about changing your personality or changing your circumstances—it's about taking care of yourself when no one is looking, so you can bring your best when people are looking.

We're constantly surprised at how many leaders believe they are the exception to this rule. We often ask leaders, "What are two or three activities that energize you and help you lead better?"

The most common answer?

"Ahhhhh..."

Long pause.

"Well, you know. That's a good question."

Longer pause.

"I enjoy walking the dog."

Really? Following an animal around and picking up their excrement is an activity that gives you the fuel you need to be an effective leader? No wonder the employee engagement statistics for your organization are so high.

You can't ignore this one. Leaders who fail to manage their fuel early in their career are often the leaders who burn out later in their career. That's why it's called "burnout."

Want to hear something shocking? If you burn out, it's your fault. We know that sounds harsh, but it's true. When a leader burns out, they rarely blame the right person. They'll often blame organizational turnover, needy clients, or the economy. They'll say things like, "I just didn't have anyone on the team I could trust."

I've known of only one leader who burned out and blamed the right person. My friend, Wes Butler, works for a sizable nonprofit in Dallas. In early 2020, he raised his hand and let everyone in the organization know he was experiencing burnout.

He had plenty of circumstances in his life to blame. Work stuff. Home stuff. Health stuff. The list was long. However, when he stood up at a staff meeting to announce he was taking some time off, guess who he blamed? Himself.

"I neglected managing my fuel."

He took about twelve weeks off. He read. He journaled. He

rested. He met with other people. He confronted some patterns in his life that were feeding a generally critical and negative outlook that he'd developed over time. The result? He came back to his career stronger and healthier than ever.

That's outstanding leadership (by Wes and his employer for letting a valued team member take some time to recalibrate).

But that doesn't have to be *your* story. Wes would tell you, "Don't follow in my footsteps." He would encourage you to begin managing your fuel now, so you don't burn out later.

It's not your boss's job or your team's job to give you the fuel you need. It's your job. So start now to develop rhythms that allow you to bring your best to your team.

We'll pick up this topic in more detail later in Chapter 7.

THE MOST IMPORTANT THING YOU BRING TO YOUR TEAM

It's not your creative ideas, work ethic, experience, knowledge, sense of humor, or baking skills. Never mind—baking skills are clutch. There are not many problems in life that a delicious baked good won't solve. Am I right, or am I right?

Sorry, I digress. The most important thing you bring to your team is your positive energy.

Now, if you are on the pessimistic side of the spectrum, hearing that your energy is the most important thing you bring to your team probably frustrates you. I get it. As a former CPA, I know what it's like to be a pessimist.

The point we're trying to make is this: regardless of where you land in the optimistic versus pessimistic spectrum, everyone can choose positivity and optimism. Positivity might be easier for some people, but it's possible for everyone.

When strong leaders gather, the room is typically full of purpose, optimism, and energy. Even in the most difficult situations, true leaders offer solutions (not problems) and keep the team moving forward. Negative, overly critical, pessimistic people often are not invited at all or over time, lose their place at the table.

Bringing energy doesn't mean you have to change your personality or temperament. It means you...

...seek to be a good improv partner.

...are thoughtful about what your body language is communicating.

...manage your fuel.

...and be you. Unless you can be a rainbow-puking unicorn. Then be a rainbow-puking unicorn.

Energetic and optimistic people communicate they are *all in*, and therefore, it's easy for them to stand out.

CHAPTER 3

GRATITUDE

A LESSON LEARNED IN BOCONÓ

Travel opens your eyes to the vastness of our world, the complexity of people, and the common humanity we share across the globe. It doesn't matter if it's a trip to Paris, Prague, or Punxsutawney. The location isn't as important as the trip itself.

When I was a young man, I visited Venezuela. I flew into the capital city of Caracas but quickly made my way to a small mountain town by the name of Boconó.

The mountains were breathtaking, and the coffee was delicious. Google it. The pictures are better than anything I'll say here.

One of the most incredible things I learned about in Venezuela was the afternoon nap, or "siesta" in Spanish.

Yes. It's a thing.

I'd work in the morning. I would eat a meal with others at lunch.

I'd rest. Remember rest? It's wonderful. I'd get up an hour later and go back to work. Glory! It's the only way to live, and the fact that we've yet to adopt this practice in the States is tragic.

I was also introduced to a new diet. Arepas! Simply delicious.

But the best thing about travel is not the food, the landscape, or the new traditions and customs. It's the people. In Boconó, I had the privilege of meeting a coffee bean farmer named Issac. He is still the coolest "old man" I've ever met. He wore an old fedora and adored his grandson, who was no older than two.

He didn't have worldly wealth, but he was more hospitable than any person I had ever met. He fed us, gave us a coffee (of course), and even offered a bed for me to take a nap. (Again, the napping. Why have we not made this a part of our "new normal"?)

Issac (and the nation of Venezuela) made a lasting impression on me. And since that trip to Boconó, I've visited Haiti twice, St. Lucia, Burundi, Rome, Venice, Istanbul, Greece, Scotland, and a second trip to beautiful Venezuela. With each trip, I'm always a tad shocked that one of the predominant emotions I feel after traveling is *gratitude*. However, upon reflection, this makes sense. One of the primary drivers of gratitude is perspective. Travel gives you perspective, and that perspective produces gratitude.

Why am I talking about gratitude in a book designed to help you become a better professional? It's because gratitude—*authentic* gratitude—is rare. It's rare in the world at large, and therefore it's probably rare in your organization.

The key to authentic gratitude isn't travel. But if you're looking for a perspective shift, it's not a bad idea. The key to authentic gratitude is adjusting your perspective.

GRATITUDE IS BEST SERVED SINCERELY

We can all agree that the only thing worse than ingratitude is insincere or inauthentic gratitude. It's better to not say anything at all than to attempt conjuring up an emotion that just ain't there. Mainly because there is absolutely no way you will get away with it.

The difference between genuine gratitude and contrived gratitude is easy to identify. Everyone can spot a con or a fraud. (That is, unless the con is *reeealllly* good—think Frank Abagnale, the con man played by Leonardo DiCaprio in that *Catch Me If You Can* movie that's always playing on TV.)

Well, be encouraged. I'm not asking you to con your way up the corporate ladder. I don't want you to be inauthentic or insincere. I want you to be honest about how you feel, and not pander to anyone.

You're probably thinking, *Okay, I've got it. Perspective first. Gratitude second. I don't want to be a fraud either. And maybe I need to book a trip to Boconó, but expressing gratitude at work is not easy. Have you met some of my teammates?*

No, we haven't met some of your teammates, but we hear you. Why is it so difficult to consistently express gratitude, especially at work? We see at least two reasons. So before we share a few ideas on how you can develop a reputation for sincere gratitude, let's unpack the two common barriers that often get in the way.

IT'S EASIER TO FOCUS ON PROBLEMS

If you've ever parented (or even taken care of a nephew or friend's child), you know that kids tend to complain a lot. It's rare that a child approaches an adult or caregiver and says, "Hey, you're great. Thanks for letting me live here rent-free. It fits my budget."

This never happens.

The average child is a lot like the average employee. They take much for granted, and complaining about problems is a standard, almost involuntary, action.

As Hara Estroff Marano said so well, "Our capacity to weigh negative input so heavily most likely evolved for a good reason—to keep us out of harm's way. From the dawn of human history, our very survival depended on our skill at dodging danger. The brain developed systems that would make it unavoidable for us not to notice danger and thus, hopefully, respond to it."[11]

I understand this full well, but as a parent, I still get discouraged when my kids fixate on a problem but fail to acknowledge that some things are awesome. That's when I get bothered. It's a desire for improvement without recognition that our life is not *that* bad. And I am less likely to be open to the ideas or requests of the child who does not acknowledge the positive aspects.

So it goes at work. It is that simple.

Yes. Your team leader sees the issues. She's not dumb. She doesn't need another employee who has a keen and expert abil-

---

11   Hara Estroff Marano, "Our Brain's Negative Bias," *Psychology Today*, June 20, 2003, https://www.psychologytoday.com/us/articles/200306/our-brains-negative-bias.

ity to spot problems. You'll learn more about this in Chapter 5 (Resourcefulness).

Automatically spotting problems and being ungrateful for the good parts of work will not make you unique among your peers. It will make you normal, which is no great accomplishment. As Dr. Seuss said, "Why fit in when you were meant to stand out?" Let's start moving away from normal.

One reason people struggle with genuine gratitude is that it's easier to focus on spotting problems than it is to focus on what's going well. Let's discuss one other barrier.

I'M RON BURGUNDY?

The second barrier to gratitude is the fact that we all have a bit of Ron Burgundy in us. We think we're "kind of a big deal." We believe our team leader should be coming by *our* desk to tell us how great we are, how much we add to the bottom line, and how valuable we are to the organization and its mission.

And maybe they should. However, worrying about what other people *should* be doing doesn't inspire change—it increases frustration. Don't worry about what your team leader should be doing. Worry about what you can control.

Team leadership is often a thankless job. You'd probably be surprised to know how many complaints your team leader hears and how little gratitude. Pressure from above and complaints from underneath. Sound fun?

Now, you might be thinking, *Of course, she gets complaints;*

there's a lot that sucks around here. Plus, she's the leader. She's empowered to fix the problems, so she needs to hear them.

Good point. Let's discuss that.

"I deserve" and "they should" are enemies of perspective and gratitude. And here's the paradox of it all.

When you feel like you deserve something, you won't be grateful when you get it. Know why? When you feel like you deserve something, you've already *taken* that thing into your possession (metaphorically). You will never appreciate something that's been given to you when you've already taken it.[12]

Read that again.

If you feel like you deserve a bonus for increasing profitability on a particular sale. You won't be grateful when you get it. If you feel like you deserve a visit from the CEO for closing the Vandelay Industries account. You won't be grateful when you get it.

Gratitude is not the outcome of events falling in line with expectations. Gratitude is the outcome of a proper perspective, regardless of what you're experiencing. Expressed gratitude is rare because most people lack the proper perspective.

We are much too concerned with our rights and far too dismissive of our responsibilities. Be obsessed with your responsibilities, and you'll see yourself granted more rights. This will help you stand out by showing you're *all in.*

---

12 Andy Stanley, "Give Thanks: An Attitude of Gratitude," November 23, 2020, YouTube video, https://youtu.be/U7aneTHx2iw.

Look, you might be Ron Burgundy. You might really be a big deal. If you've read this far, you're the kind of person who wants to be better. That's rare.

But keeping perspective and expressing gratitude is a daily grind. You don't slip into gratitude. Gratitude is a conscious pursuit. It's kind of like eating healthy, staying fit, or anything else that's worthwhile. Ever notice that the things that bring us good are hard to get? If it were easy, everyone would do it.

The ease of focusing on the negative and your bent toward self-ishness often get in the way of regularly expressing gratitude. How can you overcome these barriers and stand out? How can you do this genuinely? How can you harness the energy that gratitude provides?

We have three ideas.

IDEA #1: MAKE AND KEEP A LIST

If you are already rolling your eyes, hang with us. We suggest you create a gratitude list. It's not a terrible idea, but we know how it goes. After about three or four items, the list ends up sounding like a three-year-old's prayer. "Thank you for toothpaste. Thank you for sunshine. Thank you for watermelons. Thank you for yogurt. Thank you for light sabers."

Again, not a terrible idea, but this is not the kind of list we want you to make and keep. The list we're talking about is different— it requires two steps. We'll explain.

Step one: make and keep a list of the good things about your current workplace. The things that don't suck.

Here are some things at my current job that don't suck:

- They pay me every two weeks (this makes grocery shopping much easier).
- I have an excellent 401(k) program.
- I get three weeks of paid vacation (one more year, and it's four weeks!).
- I have holidays off (this is a modern-day privilege—read some history, your perspective will change, and gratitude will rise).
- I get weekends off (again, a historical anomaly).
- Medical benefits make wellness check-ups for the kids much cheaper.
- I have dental/vision coverage.
- My coworkers are friendly team players.
- My boss trusts me.

Okay, that's enough. You get the idea.

Even if you think some things suck at work, and even if you think your boss should be dealing with these sucky things more quickly and efficiently, it's important to keep in mind what's good about work. It helps to maintain a proper perspective.

If you are mindful of what's good, you can be thankful for it. You can express that thankfulness to your boss, and keep the bad in proper perspective. All of this benefits your career.

Step two: make and keep a list of the people who have helped you out.

The reason this list is so important is that no one is successful alone. No. One. This includes you.

Remain mindful of *who* has helped you get to where you are today. We know you think you'll never forget, but you will. Because as you grow in your career, this list gets really long, you get really old, and your memory gets really bad.

When you get a new job, write a note of thanks to the person who taught you how to interview well.

After a promotion, write a note to the coach who taught you to be consistent.

When you read a great book and get promoted, remember the authors! We'd love to hear from you. (Half-joking).

You get the idea. Make a list. Keep a list. When things happen, thank someone.

IDEA #2: SAY IT BEFORE YOU FEEL IT

Author Andy Stanley once said that "unexpressed gratitude communicates ingratitude."[13] That's worth underlining and printing on a coffee mug.

If you want to stand out and show you're *all in*, figure out a way

---

13 Stanley, "Give Thanks."

to *be* grateful and then *communicate* thankfulness. Regularly. Expressed gratitude will make you shine like a diamond in the rough.

Gratitude, like optimism, can be a challenge to express when you don't feel it. Again, I'm not asking you to be inauthentic. But I do want to point out something that's true about humans and their emotions.

Often it feels like our emotions are running the show. They are captaining the ship of our behavior. But that isn't always true. Sometimes, your actions can impact your emotions. Have you never noticed that sometimes when you start talking about positive things, suddenly, your entire outlook on life changes? Have you ever noticed how calm and peaceful you feel after a good laugh (or a good cry)?

This is why our second idea is to say it before you feel it. We know that practicing gratitude can help you feel more grateful. We don't want you to miss out on the opportunity to express gratitude while waiting for your emotions to change.

If you want to bring energy, if you want to stand out by showing you're *all in*, simply say thank you, and often. Don't wait to *feel* thankful.

One of the best parents I know taught their kids something called the "Triple Thank You" rule. I've ripped it off and taught this rule to my kids too.

Here's how it works: let's say your child's been invited to go to dinner with a friend and their family. The Triple Thank You rule means that you want your child to say thank you at the beginning of the excursion, during the middle of the excursion, and at the end of the excursion.

When your child gets picked up: "Thank you, Mr. Martin, for inviting me to dinner with you all."

During the dinner: "Mr. Martin, this is fun. Thank you again for inviting me."

After dinner: "Thank you, Martin family, for inviting me to dinner!"

We're telling you, when kids do this, it blows your mind. As it turns out, this is an excellent rule for work-life too.

Here's how you could use the Triple Thank You rule at work. Let's say you have your annual review on Wednesday. You could mention to your boss as you leave Tuesday: "Thanks for taking the time for me tomorrow. I'm looking forward to it."

On Wednesday, as you finish up (regardless of what happens), you say: "Thank you for the time. I appreciate your insight. It's super helpful."

And on Thursday, as you leave work, you say: "Just wanted to thank you again for yesterday; it was great to gain some perspective and hear more about how I can add value around here. I'm still thinking about what you said and can't wait to get going on much of it."

Sound like too much? Well, let's remember that all your boss hears is complaints. So how many "thanks" do you think it will take to outweigh all those complaints?

According to the great Marcus Buckingham (*Nine Lies About Work*), it takes three to five positive comments to outweigh a negative one. So the answer is: a lot.

Overcommunication is good. Especially positive overcommunication.

Don't worry, we've yet to meet a boss who gets too much sincere gratitude. Sure, there are plenty of frauds and suck-ups. They are a dime a dozen and quickly dismissed.

But remember. That's not you. You've done the hard work of gaining perspective. Now all you need is the intentional work of expressing your authentic gratitude regularly.

Here are other regular business times to express thanks:

- Quarterly meetings
- Birthdays
- Company milestones
- Individual milestones
- Holidays
- Upon completion of a big project/event
- When you receive an award
- And really, when someone does *anything* for you

IDEA #3: LOOK THROUGH THE WINDOW AND INTO THE MIRROR

Jim Collins is famous for the mirror/window principle. Ever

heard of it? Here's how it goes: great leaders look in a mirror when things go wrong, and they look out the window when things go well. Clever, huh?

When someone recognizes you for an achievement, thank everyone around you. When things go sideways, blame yourself.

You definitely hear this in post-game press conferences. A head coach who just got beat by three touchdowns says something like, "That's on me. I didn't have the team ready. Bad coaching."

That's looking in a mirror.

Sure, he could blame the quarterback who threw the interceptions. He could look over at his defensive coordinator and say, "I don't know, he runs the defense. Roy, what'd you do wrong? Tell 'em." That's terrible leadership. No one wants to play for that coach.

Alternatively, when a great coach has a triumphant win, he will say, "It's the players. They do the work. They make the plays. I'm proud of the way they performed today."

That's looking through a window. That's good leadership. Everyone wants to play for that coach.

Alabama's iconic football coach, Bear Bryant, considered by many to be the greatest coach of all time, once said, "If anything goes bad, I did it. Anything goes semi-good, we did it. If anything goes really well, then you did it. That's all it takes to get people to win football games for you."

Boom. That's it.

Look through the window when things go well. Look for the people who made it happen. Be mindful. Have a proper perspective of your role and the role of those who surround you. Thank everyone you see.

AN EASY WAY TO STAND OUT

All people are just like you. This includes your boss. She wants to surround herself with people who bring her life, make her happy, and make her life easier and more fun. And she's the boss, so she gets to decide who is in the room and who isn't. I'm telling you, she's going to choose grateful people. It's just the way it is.

Do the hard work of gaining perspective, and gratitude will well up inside of you. You will be authentic and honest. You will be genuinely grateful. It's impossible not to arrive at gratitude when you take perspective. It's hard, but it's worth it.

Once you've done that hard work, the rest is easy. Then all you must do is the intentional work of expressing that feeling that you've discovered.

If you want to stand out, then you need to show you're *all in*. Expressing gratitude is a simple way to bring positive energy to your team and get noticed along the way.

COMPETENCE

RESOURCEFULNESS

DILIGENCE

PRODUCTIVITY

PART 2

DILIGENCE

THE WAY YOU APPROACH YOUR WORK WITH *CARE* AND *PERSISTENCE*

CHAPTER 4

COMPETENCE

MOVEMENT REQUIRES TRUST

"Do you want to do a trust fall?" Even though that is one of the strangest things one man has ever said to another group of men, it happened to us multiple times. Rob Barry, a friend, loves trust falls more than any human we know.

What's a trust fall? A trust fall is a team-building exercise where you deliberately fall, trusting the other members of your team to catch you. Typically, it involves you standing on a coffee table or a chair and falling backward into the arms of your team.[14] It's not really a life-or-death situation. It's not Navy Seal training, but it does work. You do trust your team a bit more after the exercise.

Why did someone invent the trust fall? Two reasons.

Because they knew for any team to function well, the individual

---

14 If you are ever having a bad day, just head on to YouTube and type in "trust fall fails." Your bad day will end almost immediately.

team members must trust one another. They must have a firm belief in the reliability, truth, ability, and strength of one another.

And second, because while talking about trust is easy, building trust is a challenge. Most teams do not face life-or-death situations every day, so it's difficult to build trust quickly and efficiently. Trust falls were designed to help speed up the process.

The key to career advancement is trust. Not experience, not degrees, not looks, not height, and not the number of leather-bound books you have on your bookshelf. Trust is the ticket to career advancement.

As you start your career, an important question for you to answer is, *How can I effectively prove to others I'm trustworthy?*

You know you're trustworthy. Your parents know you're trustworthy. Your grandma knows you're trustworthy. Your team leader and peers, however, not so much.

If you do not understand how to effectively build trust, your career will stall or move much slower than you want. You don't want this. We don't want this for you.

BUT WHAT'S THE CONNECTION TO COMPETENCY?

In 2006, Stephen M. R. Covey released *The Speed of Trust: The One Thing That Changes Everything.*

He broke trust down into two basic components: character and competency. We find this very helpful and relevant to our conversation. Most of the aspiring leaders we meet understand the role character plays in building and maintaining trust. We all have had a relationship go south because the other person did not have good character, which made it impossible to trust them.

Since the importance of character goes without saying, we want to invest the majority of this chapter talking about competency. Most of the aspiring leaders we meet don't seem to understand the role competency plays in building and maintaining trust. We want to change that.

You have a higher risk of missing a promotion due to competency issues, not character issues. The number one question your team leader is asking of you is not, *Are you a person of good character?* It's, *Do you have the necessary ability, knowledge, and skills to be successful in this organization?"*

Good character is assumed; competency must be proven. As an emerging leader, the fastest way to build trust is through competency.

There are three simple ways to begin proving your competence to those around you. Take steps in these three areas, and you will begin to prove your competence to others and communicate you are *all in.*

IDEA #1: UNDERSTAND THE CORE COMPETENCIES OF YOUR JOB

As I mentioned in Chapter 1 (Motivation), I studied accounting in college. During my third year, I had to take an auditing course. I earned a B in the class, which technically means I had an above-average understanding of the subject. The truth:

I crammed for every test and faked my way through the class discussions. I didn't understand the subject matter any better than I understand how a gas refinery works.

Fast forward one year. It was time to find a full-time job and send out résumés. For some reason, I decided I would make auditing my career. I sent out six résumés to six different accounting firms and received one offer. College was a success. It prepared me for my future. I had become a professional accountant!

When I showed up for my new hire training, I started to panic. Come to find out, my employer expected me to remember what I learned in my auditing class. I was shocked. How could they do this? I took that class over twelve months ago!

What I know now that I didn't know then is the huge difference between cramming to pass a class and honestly understanding the subject matter. My academic strategy in college was basically "fake it till you make it." Pay attention, write down notes, memorize various things, do the homework, stay up late the night before a big test, and then move on to the next class.

Unfortunately, while this strategy worked in the short term, it didn't help me in the long term. My employer needed me to *understand* auditing, not just be able to cram for and pass an auditing test.

One of the fastest ways to build trust is through competence. If you can do your job and do it well, your team leader will trust you with more and more. The reward for a "job well done" is the opportunity to do more excellent work.

Needless to say, my first year was rough. I don't know if I've ever felt more incompetent in my life. I would often ask myself, "Didn't you get a B in auditing? If so, why is this so difficult for you?" Shaming for behavior change wasn't super helpful.

I'll talk more about my first few years out of college toward the end of this chapter, but suffice to say now, it took me longer than normal to gain my EDGE as an auditor. It took my bosses longer than normal to trust me. Was it because I had questionable character? Fortunately, no. The reason it took my bosses longer than normal to trust me was due to my lack of competence.

The point I'm trying to illustrate is this: focusing intently on understanding and executing the fundamentals of your job is the fastest way to build trust with your team leaders. Don't approach your job like I approached college. If there is something you don't understand about your job, ask.

> "I've been creating these reports for the past few months, and I realized, I don't know why we create them and who reads them. Will you help me understand why we create these reports?"

> "I've noticed that we rework our marketing campaign every sixty days. This seems like a lot of extra work—can you help me understand why we do this?"

> "Every week I'm supposed to make these phone calls, but I'm not sure why I can't just send this information out as an email. Will you help me better understand why we think a phone call is better?"

Anytime you admit you don't understand something, it's humbling. We see many emerging leaders fail to truly understand the fundamentals of their job because they are too embarrassed to ask "why?"

When you ask "why" questions, you will be viewed as diligently curious, not surprisingly ignorant. Every organization is unique. Every organization has its own way of doing things. No one comes into an organization and immediately knows everything. Everyone experiences a learning curve. You can't control how steep the learning curve will be for you, but you can control how fast you move through the learning curve by remaining curious, seeking to understand, and working to excel at the core competencies of your job.

Gaining mastery over the key portions of your job proves your competence and gives you an EDGE.

IDEA #2: UNDERSTAND YOUR ORGANIZATION'S CULTURE

You can ask the magic mirror on the office bathroom wall, *What is the buzziest corporate buzzword of them all?* You may expect any of these: paradigm, framework, scale, synergy, or pivot. But the magic mirror knows better...it's culture.

Over the last ten years, few topics have become more popular for leaders than culture.

Culture is the accumulation of behaviors, motivated by core values, that characterize a group of people.[15] Any organization with more than one person has a culture. Leaders cannot "create"

---

15   George Barna, *Revolution* (Carol Stream, IL: Tyndale House Publishers, 2005).

a culture any more than they can create air. Cultures just exist when people get together.

Leaders can try to shape, mold, and influence their culture. That's why it's such a buzzy topic. There are thousands of leadership gurus and consultants helping leaders develop healthy, strong, diverse, inclusive, sustainable cultures.

There is a well-known quote by Peter Drucker: "Culture eats strategy for breakfast." In many ways, Peter was right. Culture, for most organizations, is more important than strategy. Strategy is *how* you are going to accomplish a specific goal. Culture is the people who will be responsible for executing the strategy. If the people executing the strategy don't understand the goal, communicate well, appreciate one another, and know their roles, the strategy will not be successfully executed.

Thus, culture eats strategy for breakfast. Why breakfast and not lunch or dinner? We have no clue, but his point was made.

We don't want to turn this book into a resource on culture. But we want to make sure we're all on the same page with this word because understanding the culture at your organization will help you build trust and stand out.

After you begin to understand how to do what you are paid to do, we suggest making your next step understanding your organization's agreed-upon behaviors. Remember, that's the keyword when it comes to culture: *behavior*. How do the people in your organization act?

It's important to study behavior, not posters, marketing brochures, or web pages. Culture is lived and experienced, not merely talked about.

As you study your organization, keep your eyes and ears open for the following items.

1. *Phrases that get repeated.* Although culture is lived, not spoken, you do need to pay attention to phrases that get repeated so you can stress-test them and determine if a pithy phrase is just corporate mumbo-jumbo or truly an aspect of your culture. As you sit in your team meetings or your organization's all-staff meetings, listen for phrases that get repeated and then see if you can find evidence that people are regularly acting on that phrase. Doing this will help you learn so much about your organization's culture (or give you something to talk about over lunch with your coworkers).

2. *What behavior is celebrated.* Again, during your team meetings or all-staff meetings, observe and notice who gets celebrated. Why? Leaders reward behaviors they want to see repeated in others. Celebrations are cultural clues.

3. *What behavior is not tolerated.* These clues are a little more difficult to uncover because most organizations keep reprimands and disciplinary action hush-hush. However, it's not impossible, and observing what behaviors are not tolerated provides great clues.

Why study culture? Because of "institutional knowledge"—the combination of experience, data, expertise, and information possessed by an employee. It's knowing the *ins and outs* of your organization. The way things really get done. It's having context and understanding not only your team or department but also the entire organization.

Institutional knowledge is an asset. The sooner you begin to accumulate this asset, the faster you communicate to your leaders that you're *all in*. Understanding your organization communicates that you are *for* your organization—that you understand you play a role in the larger team, which you humbly and respectfully desire to learn more about.

Studying and understanding the nuances of your organizational culture proves your competence and helps you stand out by showing you are *all in*.

IDEA #3: UNDERSTAND YOUR INDUSTRY

In the late 1990s, Blockbuster Video had over 9,000 locations, 84,000 employees (including one of your authors, Adam, thank you very much), and 65 million members. If you and your friends wanted to rent a movie, you drove to Blockbuster because that was pretty much the only option you had.

In 1999, Netflix showed up offering an entirely new way to rent movies. Instead of driving to a physical store, you could simply log onto their website, select a few movies, and two days later, they showed up in your mailbox. Yes, you had to make your entertainment choices two days in advance. However, it saved consumers time (you didn't have to drive to the store only to realize *Jerry Maguire* still wasn't in stock) and money (the movies were cheaper to rent, and you didn't have to pay late fees if you kept the movies a few extra days).

Netflix enjoyed tremendous growth from 1999 to 2011. They were *the* player in movie rentals. Blockbuster was all but gone in 2011, six years away from bankruptcy. Netflix had completely disrupted the market, and they were winning the home entertainment game.

Then, they did something crazy. Netflix completely changed its business model. In 2011, they began offering two different subscription options: a traditional DVD plan and a new streaming plan. Not only did they offer two subscriptions, but they also hiked up their prices and said they believed streaming was the future. Everyone laughed at them, and their stock price dropped 74 percent in three months (due in part to an increase in prices). They looked like fools.

Here they were at the top of the game, one of the most recognizable brands in the world, and they had essentially knocked out their top competitor (Blockbuster). Why on earth would a company at its peak do something that looked so foolish in the short term?

Because someone (or multiple someones) at Netflix didn't just understand the core competencies of their job and the company's culture. They also understood their industry and had a strong inclination about the future.

They knew broadband infrastructure was improving and people were not going to continue making entertainment decisions two days in advance. They knew everything was moving to online and on-demand. So they decided to learn from Blockbuster and make their change early, instead of waiting until it was too late.

Looking back, Netflix's decision to focus on streaming is viewed as one of the smartest "pivots" in American business history. It would have never happened if someone *inside* the organization hadn't been looking *outside* the organization. Understanding what's going on outside the organization is a great way to stand out and show you're *all in*.

As you seek to build trust with the leaders in your organization, understanding your job, the company culture, and your industry will help.

Your organization does not exist in a vacuum, so it is good to have a general understanding of the context in which your organization exists. Here are some questions to guide you as you begin to understand your industry:

- Who are your competitors?
- What economic factors impact your organization?
- What political issues impact your organization?
- What changes in technology will impact your organization?

Attempting to answer these questions might not lead to a breakthrough idea, but it does communicate to people around you that you are thoughtful and interested in more than just your to-do list, which builds trust and shows you are *all in*. In fact, this is one of the biggest differences between a team *member* and a team *leader*. We'll discuss this in more detail in Chapter 8 (Ownership), but for now, remember this: team leaders are always thinking about more than just their personal to-do list. Learning to think and act like a team leader is vital as your career advances.

When you gain a basic understanding of your organization's industry, it communicates that you are thoughtful and forward-thinking. Competence in this area builds trust.

THIS IS THE SECRET TO YOUR FIRST PROMOTION(S)

As I mentioned above, I had to learn this lesson about competency the hard way.

When I started working as an auditor, my primary goal was to be a "good guy." I thought it would give me an advantage and help me stand out. So starting on day one, I tried to be nice to my bosses, colleagues, and clients. I focused on maintaining a positive attitude and tried my best to be a joy to others. Said another way, I focused on the character side of Covey's trust formula.

This was all fine and good until I started to do actual work. At that moment, it became clear I really didn't know what I was doing. I'm not talking about the normal "new employee" fog. I'm talking *for real*: I had no clue what I was doing. Remember, I faked my way through my auditing class in college.

After a few hard conversations with my team leaders, I realized something important. I was not hired to be a "good guy." I was hired to be a "good auditor." I was not gaining trust with the other managers and partners because they were focused on the competency side of Covey's trust formula.

Rightly or wrongly, my firm assumed everyone was a "good person." The entire firm was full of (mostly) good people. What they really needed from me was competency. They needed me to take my job more seriously.

Looking back on it now, I realize they were totally right. The partners at that accounting firm were not giving me money to brighten people's day. Can you imagine a partner calling up a client and saying this:

> Judy, we're putting Adam on this job. Don't get us wrong, he has no clue how to audit your balance sheet, and for the love of mercy, don't ask him to create a statement of cash flows. However, he's a nice guy, and he won't be mean to anyone in your office. In fact, on Fridays he brings in donuts. So, you're welcome! I look forward to doing most of the work myself when I find time.

The partners were giving me money to save them time by auditing their client's financial statements on their behalf. That's what a job is. You do work the team leader or owner can't or doesn't want to do in exchange for money. The partners assumed I had character; otherwise, they wouldn't have hired me. What they needed me to prove was my competency.

I'm grateful for the early team leaders who had those difficult conversations with me. I'm grateful they were not okay with me simply being a "good guy." I'm thankful they didn't fire me the first time I turned in questionable work. I'm grateful they were patient with me until the lightbulb came on. After a few awkward conversations, I began to focus more and more on proving my competency, and eventually, I was rewarded with a promotion.

You probably know this already, but team leaders don't hand out promotions for nothing. Promotions are handed out based on merit. Of course, there are some shady team leaders in the world who give out promotions for all the wrong reasons. If you work for one of those leaders, it's probably best to get out of that situation as soon as possible.

For the rest of you, remember, your first few promotions will not happen because you have high potential, you're a "good person," and your boss believes one day you will make a great leader. Your first few promotions will happen because your team leader trusts you. He trusts that you understand (and excel at) the core competencies of your job, that you understand your organization's culture, and that you are growing in your understanding of your organization's industry.

When you are diligent, you work hard at proving your competency because competency builds trust. Trusted people have an EDGE and totally stand out by showing they are *all in*.

CHAPTER 5

RESOURCEFULNESS

DR. PROBLEM SOLVER OR: HOW YOU LEARNED TO STOP WORRYING AND LOVE ISSUES

Remember, this part is about how diligence—careful and persistent effort—gives you an EDGE. Diligence is broken down into three components: competence (Chapter 4), resourcefulness (this chapter), and persistence (Chapter 6).

One of the fastest ways to stand out among your peers is to develop the ability to find quick and clever solutions to difficulties and issues. To not back down when you see problems. To not be afraid of thorny issues. To even get a little excited when difficulties arise. A great way to stand out among your peers is to pretend your career is being featured in a film called *Dr. Problem Solver or: How You Learned to Stop Worrying and Love Issues.*[16]

I'd totally watch that movie.

---

16 A nod to the 1964 Stanley Kubrick film *Dr. Strangelove or: How I Learned to Stop Worrying and Love the Bomb* (London: Stanley Kubrick Productions, 1964), which satirized the Cold War fears.

To that end, let's keep moving and talk about how you can develop the skill of resourcefulness.

NO DUMPING

Picture a scenario where you're trying to finish up your work on a Friday afternoon but can't stop being distracted by your over-flowing trash can. Eventually, you give in and decide to empty it yourself, but on your way to the break room, you pass by your boss's office and decide to pop in and ask about her weekend plans. Then you have what you think is a fantastic idea: you start to dump the garbage on your boss's desk, saying, "Here, will you take care of this for me so I can get back to work?" You thank her and return to your desk, thinking, *Aren't bosses great?!*

You would never do that, right? You would never take your trash can and dump it on your boss's desk. So why do we share that ridiculous scenario?

Well, because we're pretty sure you do something similar to your team leader, and you don't even know it.

If you've ever gone to your team leader and pointed out a problem *without* offering a solution, then, metaphorically speaking, you dumped trash on their desk.

The client hasn't gotten us the back-up we need, so I can't finish auditing this section.

Our reporting system doesn't work very well. It's clunky and slow. I wish we had a better one.

You asked me to finish this project, but Sarah just went home. She's sick. What should I do?

That meeting is boring.

Our referral system doesn't work very well.

We don't know your team leader, but it's safe to assume they probably don't want you dumping trash on their desk. Real or metaphorical.

AN *EASY* WAY TO GET FIRED (OR PROMOTED)

Problems are hard. They require effort, brainpower, and fortitude. Most of the time when you encounter a problem, the first thought that crosses your mind is, *How can I get out of this?*

Don't beat yourself up. Part of this reaction is biological, and part of it is learned.

From a biological standpoint, this is the way your brain is wired. In a 2018 study from the University of British Columbia, it was determined that our brains are hardwired to find laziness attractive.[17]

Matthieu Boisgontier, who authored the study, has this to say: "Conserving energy has been essential for humans' survival, as it allowed us to be more efficient in searching for food and shelter, competing for sexual partners, and avoiding predators."

---

17   Chrissy Sexton, "The Brain's Instinct to Conserve Energy Makes People Lazy," *Earth.com*, accessed June 21, 2022, https://www.earth.com/news/brain-lazy-conserve-energy/.

We are *huge* fans of conserving energy. Seriously, you should see David on vacation. I promise you would say, "How can he just sit there doing nothing for such a long period of time?" If the Olympics had a "do nothing" competition, David would be a strong contender for a medal.

Back to the subject. Solving problems is the exact opposite of conserving energy.

From a learned behavior standpoint, you have grown accustomed to outsourcing your problems. The global economy exists because people have problems in their lives they cannot solve on their own (or do not want to solve on their own).

Every organization solves a problem:

INDUSTRY	PROBLEM IT SOLVES
Medical	People get sick
Food	People need food to survive
Entertainment	People get bored and want to relax
Gyms	People eat and sit around too much and need to exercise so they don't need more medical services
Computer	People want to write, learn, and communicate without using typewriters, going to the library to research Mount Everest's height, calling someone to book travel plans, or writing letters
Construction	People don't want to camp every day, use an outhouse, or work outside
Automobile	People need to travel and don't want to ride horses

As a member of the global economy, you have learned to pay people to solve your problems. Problem avoidance is what being a "consumer" is all about. As Donald Miller says, "People buy solutions to internal problems."[18] That is what all good capitalists do.

However, problem avoidance is not what makes a good teammate, and it won't give your career an EDGE.

At work, when you point out a problem *without* offering a solution, you are saying, "I've got something on my to-do list that I can't figure out, so here—you figure it out for me."

If you are a person who takes items from your to-do list and puts them on your team leader's to-do list, sooner or later, you will find yourself without a to-do list to manage.

Do you smell what we're cooking there?

Said another way, one of the easiest ways to get fired is to get in the habit of putting items on your team leader's to-do list.

Thankfully, the opposite is also true. If you prove to be a person who *removes* items from your team leader's to-do list, that's an easy way to get promoted. That type of behavior is one of the quickest ways to stand out.

WHY LEADERS EXIST

Your organization exists because problems exist, and leaders in your organization exist because problems exist. Leaders are the real problem experts in both the global economy and your organization.

---

18   Donald Miller, *Building a StoryBrand: Clarify Your Message So Customers Will Listen* (New York: HarperCollins Leadership, 2017), 62.

Every single day, leaders deal with problems. But (and this is crucial) leaders are not experts at *seeing* problems; they are experts at *solving* problems.

Seeing problems doesn't make you a leader. It makes you a Karen.

Problems are easy to spot. Just ask any impatient, box-wine drinking, minivan-driving, soccer mom (a.k.a. Karen). They love "talking to managers" about the problems they see.

Solving problems makes you a leader. Many leaders spend most of their day solving problems and removing the obstacles their teams face as they try to accomplish their mission.

Problems show up every day. I cannot emphasize that enough: EVERY. DAY. It's one of the great joys of being a leader, but also one of the great annoyances.

Every day when a leader wakes up, they have no clue what trash will end up on their desk. Sometimes the problems are related to technology. Sometimes the problems are related to personnel. Sometimes they are related to the economy. Sometimes they are related to the competition. Often, they are related to fickle and needy customers.

No matter what industry you are in, where you went to college, or how much you get paid, problems show up every day, and it's the leader's job to ensure these problems get solved.

You need a new worldview for your work. You need to not just see the problems but also see practical ways to find solutions. You need to be Dr. Problem Solver.

You might be thinking, *One qualifier. What if I don't have a proposed solution? Should I still point it out?*

Sometimes, yes. For example, when you...

...realize the executive team is cheating.

...learn that there's been a breach in your customer data.

...learn there's a price-fixing scheme.

...witness racism, sexism, ageism.

When these situations arise, you need to have the courage to blow a whistle and point out a problem. In these situations, the most important thing to do is point out the problem.

There's a story about Toyota North America. They give every single person on their manufacturing line a "kill switch." The "kill switch" gives anyone on the line the power to shut down the line. The only instruction given is this: "if you see a problem, stop production, so we can solve it."

Why do they give everyone in the factory this power? Easy: they don't want to hide mistakes or problems. They want to bring attention to them because it's an opportunity to improve a process.

It's a part of the Toyota culture to celebrate problem spotters.

In the situations mentioned above, your organization needs a problem spotter.

Not pointing out those kinds of problems because you don't have a proposed solution isn't helpful.

So there are times when courageously pointing out a problem *is* being a leader. Don't shy away from those situations when they arise. However, for most people, those situations will be rare.

Now that we've got that qualifier out of the way, we want to throw out three ideas to help you develop the reputation of being a problem solver.

IDEA #1: VIEW EVERY PROBLEM AS AN OPPORTUNITY TO PRACTICE REAL LEADERSHIP

What bothers me most about problems is how they slow me down. I like progress. I want to move forward. Problems are like being stuck in a traffic jam, stalling on the tarmac before taking off, or waiting in line at Disney World. "Slow" is a vulgar cuss word to most people. You don't like slowing down, we don't like slowing down, and your team leader doesn't like slowing down.

We say this to empathize with the temptation you face when a problem arises. You've got tasks on your list to power through, and you don't want to slow down. A problem is inconvenient. No one wakes up in the morning saying, "Wow, I cannot wait to be slowed down by a dumpster fire of unexpected issues today!"

If you want a successful career, you need to embrace the problems you face. Don't take the easy way out and dump the problem on your team leader's desk. Take a moment and recognize the opportunity handed to you.

Every problem you face at work is an opportunity to act like a *real* leader. Remember what we said earlier: leaders spend most of their day solving problems—not playing golf—and thinking about the future.

The metaphor is overused, but we'll use it anyway. Every time you face a problem at work, it's like you just stepped into the gym. Think of solving problems like doing burpees. They hurt, but they help. Trying to solve a problem is one of the most significant ways to train as a leader. We know it hurts to slow down, but it's worth it.

One of the best teammates I ever had was a woman named Ann Piper. Ann was the director of communications at a large nonprofit. She was responsible for orchestrating all external communications for our organization. Every day she walked into our offices and had no clue what problems she would face— and there were many. She handled every problem with grace, wisdom, and only the slightest bit of cursing.

What I appreciated most about Ann was her initiative to propose solutions. Ann and I would meet up one-on-one a few times a month to discuss her work, her to-do list, and her team. They were some of the most productive one-on-one meetings I've ever had in my career. She always had an agenda and was very respectful of my time. When there was an item she wanted my feedback on, she would present the issue, and then present two or three proposed solutions.

As you heard in our all-hands-on-deck meeting this morning, we are hosting a new event on Saturday night. I'm not exactly sure how the leaders want to promote this event, but here's what I'm thinking: We draft up a short email to send out to our constituents on Thursday. Then we promote the event on Facebook Friday and Saturday. How's that plan sound?

Were all of her proposed solutions perfect? No, but that wasn't my expectation. What I appreciated most was her willingness to do the hard work of proposing solutions and giving me options. She never dumped trash on my desk. She never wanted to put anything on my to-do list. She was a dream teammate.

So the next time you face a problem, resist the urge to call your boss. Instead, take a deep breath and embrace the opportunity to practice leadership. If you do, then my second idea will help you brainstorm possible solutions.

IDEA #2: ASK YOURSELF AN OUTSIDE-LOOKING-IN QUESTION

Remember your high school math classes? Chances are you spent as much time daydreaming as you did learning math. After dinner, you'd sit down to do your homework, but of course, because you had been daydreaming while the teacher explained the assignment, you didn't understand the homework.

What did you do?

A. Go back to the beginning of the chapter and reread the lesson again.
B. Go back to the notes you took and remind yourself of the key concepts.

c. Call a friend and ask for tutoring.

D. None of the above.

We know it was "D." You went to the back of the book and copied the answers. That's the reason you passed math all four years in high school. Not because you exhibited a mastery of the subject. It's because the answers to your problems were in the back of the book.

You know where we're going next. But we're going to say it anyway. In real life, there are no answers in the back of the book. Go ahead. Roll your eyes. We can't see you anyway.

Most real-life problems are challenging to solve. They are tricky, thorny, and complex. The answers aren't clear. This is why problems slow you down and why you think about passing them off to your boss.

One simple way to begin thinking about solutions is to ask yourself an outside-looking-in question. This is a question designed to help you gain perspective and trick your brain into coming up with possible solutions.

Here are some examples:

How would my team leader solve this problem?

How would a great leader solve this problem?

If I was Robert Neville (the lead character in I Am Legend*), how would I solve this problem?*

The outside-looking-in question taps into that innate ability everyone has to solve someone else's problem faster and better than we can solve our problems. You know what we mean.

Think about your sister's life. You know *exactly* what her problem is and how to fix it, right? It's easy. Her real problem is that she doesn't listen to you. If she would just listen to you, then she wouldn't be mooching off your parents and driving that ridiculous car, and...anyway, you get what we mean.

Outside-looking-in questions are a great tool to help you embrace and solve problems rather than passing them off to someone else.

One additional comment before we move on to our third idea. Keep in mind that early on in the problem-solving process, your number one goal is to get a list of *possible* solutions. You are not looking for the silver bullet. You are looking for possibilities.

When you present possible solutions to your team leader, the ball is now in their court to decide if they want to try one of your solutions or implement one of their own.

This is about the *process*. The process of communicating both a problem and a proposed solution is the win. The win isn't being right. The win is being thoughtful.

So let's say you've encountered a problem. You've resisted the urge to pass the buck and decided instead to embrace the opportunity to practice real leadership. You've asked yourself a few outside-looking-in questions, and you now have a list of possible solutions. You engage in a conversation with your boss, and you present the problem *and* offer two possible solutions. Your boss thanks you for your ideas but rejects your proposed solutions and asks you to solve the problem another way. What do you do in that situation? We got you—let's discuss our third idea.

IDEA #3: TRUST THE PROCESS

Just because you went through the hard work of proposing a solution doesn't mean your boss will select it. *When* this happens (not *if*), don't fret. Follow the lead of the former Philadelphia 76ers general manager, Sam Hinkie.

Back in 2013, the Philadelphia 76ers were rebuilding their basketball team. During this rebuilding phase, Hinkie would often talk about "the process."[19] As a leader, he let the team and the fans know with absolute clarity that the next few years were going to be a wild ride. They would see progress, and they would see setbacks. They would have moments of overperforming and moments of underperforming. What Hinkie was basically telling the fanbase was not to fixate on the record or standings, but to look at the big picture and ask, *Is the team getting better? Are they moving toward being a championship contender? Are they moving in the right direction?*

Early in your career, you are like the 2013 Philadelphia 76ers. You are growing, learning, and preparing. Your parents may believe you are ready to be the CEO even though you've only been out of school for two years, and before your current job, you worked as a lifeguard at summer camp. We want to be your

---

19   Max Rappaport, "The Definitive History of 'Trust the Process,'" *Bleacher Report*, August 23, 2017, https://bleacherreport.com/articles/2729018-the-definitive-history-of-trust-the-process.

friend and tell you the truth: your parents might have been stretching the truth just a bit.

You are not ready to be the CEO of your company. No one goes from president of Sigma Chi to CEO in two years.

We know what you're thinking: *What about Mark Zuckerberg? He was ready.* Probably not. How can we say that? Because no twenty-something has ever been "ready" to lead a multi-million dollar, publicly traded company. Don't confuse market success with leadership readiness.

What we're saying is this: when you face a problem, trust the process, and remain fully committed to finding creative solutions to the challenges your team faces each day. Then if your proposed solution is not chosen, do these three things:

1. Give yourself credit for not dumping trash on your team leader's desk. That's a big deal and a step in the right direction.

2. Study your organization and your team leader's solution. Observe what went right (and wrong) as the solution was implemented. If you have time, ask your boss how they came to their conclusion and why. You can learn so much from your team leader by learning how they think about problems.

3. Own your team leader's solution like it was your own. This is a great way to show you are *all in*.

Remember, just because your team leader didn't choose your solution doesn't mean you aren't smart or a good leader. It just means you're "in process." You're still learning about the company's culture and how your boss thinks about problem-solving. That's part of your journey as a leader. Your ideas not being chosen don't have to be a hit to your core identity.

Own it like it was your idea and implement the proposed solution with positivity and energy.

Keep in mind that leadership can be very lonely, and being punched in the face day after day, solving problem after problem, can be exhausting. Having someone who is not afraid to jump in and get their hands dirty is a huge help to a leader. So a quick and simple way to attract your team leader's attention is to be a problem solver. Period. The more you exhibit the ability to think through how to solve problems critically, the quicker you gain an EDGE.

The more you view problems as an opportunity to train, the better prepared you will be when more opportunity comes your way.

The faster you learn to own solutions that are not yours and how to compromise without being bitter, the farther down the road you are on your leadership journey.

So don't dump the trash can on your team leader's desk. Take care of your own trash. Or wait for the cleaning crew. They get paid to do that kind of stuff.

CHAPTER 6

PRODUCTIVITY

THE SUCCESS YOU WILL NEVER HAVE

There is a famous quote by Wayne Gretzky: "You miss 100 percent of the shots you don't take." This is excellent to keep in mind as we wrap up our discussion on careful and persistent work.

Remember, we are asserting that Energy, Diligence, Growth, and Endurance will help you stand out by showing you're *all in*. These will give your career an EDGE.

This is the final part of the discussion on diligence. Diligence is comprised of competence (Chapter 4), resourcefulness (Chapter 5), and productivity (this chapter). Diligence gives you a chance to succeed—because you are sure to be unsuccessful if you never take the shot.

A TALE OF YOUR ORGANIZATION

We need to remind you of something—the story of *your* organization.

Yes, we have no clue who you work for, but every organization with more than one employee has a similar story.

Once upon a time, the founder of your organization had an idea.

His idea was very specific.

He had developed a product or service that he believed would solve a problem for people.

The founder acted on his idea and began performing this problem-solving activity in exchange for money, donations, or tax dollars.

The founder made people's lives just a little bit better because the founder was solving this problem.

As the founder successfully helped more and more people, he developed a favorable reputation in the marketplace.

As a result of this favorable reputation, more and more people began asking the founder to perform his problem-solving activity.

A rhythm developed: the founder would solve a customer's problem, the customer would tell their friends, and the founder would get more work.

This rhythm continued for a period of time.

The founder was encouraged. More earnings began to come the founder's way.

Life was good. Customers were happy. The founder was delighted.

But then something changed.

Finally, it got to a point where the founder could no longer perform all the work.

The founder was so focused on solving his customer's problems that *he* now had a problem that needed solving.

His problem was this: *I have more work to do than I can handle by myself.*

As he thought about his problem, he realized there were two possible solutions.

His first option? Turn work away. The upside of this decision: he wouldn't have to spend any money to solve his problem. The downside of this decision: his organization wouldn't grow.

His other option? Hire someone to help him perform the excess work. The upside of this decision: his organization would grow. The downside of this decision: it would cost money to hire an employee.

As the founder assessed his financial situation, he realized he had enough cash to hire another employee. It would be risky, but if he could take on additional customers, the extra cash flow would be enough to pay for the employee and still earn a profit.

He decided to go for option two: hire an employee.

This risky decision paid off. Big time!

The reputation of this organization continued to grow.

As a result, more work started coming in.

Sooner or later, the amount of work became so burdensome that the founder hired another employee. Then another. Then another.

This was the new rhythm: whenever there was more work to do than the founder and his employees could handle, he would hire another employee to help with the workload.

After a short time, this one-person organization grew into a twelve-person organization.

And then, one day, the founder hired *you* to help with the workload. You, the founder, and the other employees all lived happily ever after. Kind of.

IT'S CALLED WORK FOR A REASON

So why on earth did we just tell you that story?

We want to remind you of a simple truth that is easy to forget. The simple fact is: *you were hired to do work.*

Your team leader hired you to solve a problem. The problem wasn't *we need another nice person around the office to tell us jokes during team meetings and make us jealous about their exciting weekend on Instagram.*

Your boss hired you to perform activities she can't perform. (Or maybe she just doesn't want to perform herself. Kind of like why we pay for our dress shirts to get laundered. We *could* do it, but we don't want to, so we pay someone else to do it for us.)

Your organization solves problems for its customers, clients, and constituents in exchange for money.

You solve a problem for your organization in exchange for money too.

Win, win, win. Right?

Right.

SPEAKING OF RIGHT...KOBE HAD IT RIGHT

We have some *excellent* news for you. One of the simple secrets to success in life is to get stuff done.

Action.

Movement.

Progress.

Completion.

These are words that all founders, leaders, and bosses love.

If you develop the reputation of being someone who accomplishes tasks and doesn't complain while doing it, watch out. Good things are going to come your way!

The year 2020 will go down as one of the worst years in human history. It started with the tragic and untimely death of Kobe Bryant. Regardless of what you think about Kobe and his career, one thing everyone agrees on is the man worked hard. Here are a few examples of his work ethic:

- In high school, he would show up at 5:00 a.m. to practice. In high school!
- His Lakers teammates said he was always the first one to the gym, even when injured.
- He once played a game left-handed because he injured his right shoulder.
- He once began practice at 4:15 a.m. and didn't end until 11:00 a.m. He refused to leave until he made 800 shots.
- He stopped eating sugar and pizza to keep his body in shape.
- He regularly cold-called business leaders and entrepreneurs to learn from them.[20]

His work ethic and bias toward action started early in his career and stayed with him up until his last moment. It's worth noting that Kobe didn't believe he was gifted. He didn't want to be known as a "special" basketball talent. He wanted to be known as someone who worked hard. Someone who acted on his ideas.

---

20 Scott Davis and Connor Perrett, "Kobe Bryant's Work Ethic Was Unmatched, Here Are 24 Examples," *Insider,* last modified January 26, 2020, https://www.businessinsider.com/kobe-bryant-insane-work-ethic-2013-8#he-once-played-left-handed-because-he-injured-his-right-shoulder-6.

"To think of me as a person that's overachieved, that would mean a lot to me. That means I put a lot of work in and squeezed every ounce of juice out of this orange that I could."

Kobe figured out one of life's simple secrets: success generally happens when a person has a bias toward action.

For the sake of clarity, here is what's *not* a simple secret to success in life:

1. Your smarts

2. A degree from a prestigious university

3. A stacked résumé

4. Your height

5. Your looks

6. Your extroversion

7. Your ability to do a hundred push-ups a day

8. The number of social media connections or followers you have

You get the picture.

Those things we just listed out certainly won't hurt. But they are not the secret to success in life.

Action. Movement. Progress. Completion. Work on those things, and you'll find yourself standing out in no time.

Here are three ideas we believe will help you become a productivity wizard.

IDEA #1: DEVELOP A SYSTEM FOR CAPTURING IDEAS, REMINDERS, AND TASKS

You can't act on something you forget to do. Therefore, the first step in becoming a productivity genius is developing a system for capturing tasks. To that end, here are three suggestions to keep in mind:

1. *Your system should be portable.* Today's work environment is fast and flexible. Gone are the days when a leader goes to work and sits in one physical location all day. Therefore, you need a task-capturing system that is flexible enough to follow you throughout the day. If your system isn't portable, you'll end up missing critical tasks.

2. *Everything* should be in one location. We won't die on this hill, but we might spar a bit. The best task-capturing system puts everything in one place. It could be in an app like GoodNotes, Asana, Todoist, or Evernote. It could be in a Word or Google document. It could be in a journal. You can use a combination, but have one final destination for all tasks.[21] There is no perfect way to do this. Pick the one location

---

21   For example, Adam uses GoodNotes on his iPad (with the Apple Pencil) for taking notes during meetings, Todoist for capturing and tracking his tasks, and Evernote for more personal reflection and drafting of ideas. However, all task-capturing goes directly into Todoist. No exceptions. If it doesn't make it into Todoist, it doesn't get done.

that works for you, and don't deviate. The alternative to one location is either multiple locations or no location. Both of which mean you will miss something. We promise. Pick one location and use it for everything.

3. *Your system should relieve stress.* We've all experienced that "oh crap!" moment when you realize you were supposed to do something, and forgot because you failed to write it down. Those moments cause stress. The more frequently you experience those moments, the more you stress about them all the time.

You know you have the right system when it's letting very few things slip through the cracks, and your stress level is low. Your system is supposed to serve you and make your life less stressful, not more stressful.

The beauty of a good system is you never have to worry about forgetting. If you are sitting in a meeting and your boss says, "We need to remember this next time we work with this client," no worries; open up your system and write it down. You'll never have to worry about "remembering this" again.

One final thought. When in doubt, just capture it. When you catch a task or an idea, it doesn't mean you will execute it. It's better to write down a few bad ideas or "possible tasks" and delete them later than to risk forgetting them altogether.

Don't worry. You're not C. S. Lewis or Abe Lincoln. No one is going to read your journals when you die. So when an idea hits you, capture it. If you hear a to-do item discussed in a meeting, capture it. If someone gives you a reminder, capture it. Who cares if it's dumb, unnecessary, or otherwise useless? No one sees your journal or todo list but you.

IDEA #2: ALWAYS SET A DUE DATE

This is crucial. Capturing tasks and ideas is a great first step. But the real secret to action, movement, progress, and completion is assigning a due date.

Due dates are helpful for two reasons. One, they make you prioritize, and two, they awaken the Panic Monster inside you. Let us explain.

Prioritize. All tasks are not created equal. Just because something is captured on your to-do list doesn't mean you should complete it as soon as possible. Learning to prioritize tasks is crucial for keeping you focused on the right things.

Priorities are always linear. Always. You cannot have two first priorities. In fact, the word *priority* really shouldn't be spoken or written in plural. By definition, a priority is the *singular* most important thing/person/task. But this isn't a grammar lesson; it's about you progressing in your career. So let's get back to that.

If everything is important, then nothing is important. Prioritize.

Most organizations don't struggle to capture ideas and tasks; they struggle with prioritization—what needs to be done *next*.

If you don't force-rank your to-do list, you will find yourself *busy* but not *productive*. So get into the habit of looking at your to-do list and force-ranking your tasks. The goal is not busyness; the goal is productivity. Deadlines (a.k.a. due dates) help you prioritize.

As we mentioned, due dates, when used correctly, also awaken the Panic Monster inside you. Who is the Panic Monster? This idea came from Tim Urban's brilliant TED Talk titled "Inside the Mind of a Master Procrastinator." You have three characters living in your brain battling for control:

1. *The Rational Decision Maker.* This character makes sure we live a responsible and productive life. Most mature adults want this person to control their brain as often as possible.

2. *The Instant Gratification Monkey.* This character wants us to experience a life that's easy and fun. He is the reason we go on YouTube binges when we need to be doing real work or why we play an hour of Angry Birds when we need to go to sleep. Most mature adults want this person to control their brain as little as possible.

3. *The Panic Monster.* This character gets a bad rap, but in many ways, he's a hero. When the Instant Gratification Monkey has been controlling the brain for too long, the Panic Monster shows up and scares the ever-living you-know-what out of the Instant Gratification Monkey, causing him to run off into the dark recesses of your brain.

With the Instant Gratification Monkey gone, the Rational Decision Maker regains control of the brain, and you get back to work.

Most of the time, the Panic Monster is sleeping and not causing problems. However, there is one thing that always, and I mean *always*, causes the Panic Monster to awaken, and that one thing is stress.

When the brain realizes there's been a shot of adrenaline or cortisol in the body, the Panic Monster awakens and goes to work.

The Instant Gratification Monkey *hates* the Panic Monster. So when the stress of a looming deadline awakens the Panic Monster, the Instant Gratification Monkey gives up control of the brain back to the Rational Decision Maker, and all is good. Stuff gets done.

Now, sometimes the Panic Monster can scare the ever-living you-know-what out of the Rational Decision-Maker and send him off into the dark recesses of your brain too. That's called the Amygdala Hijack,[22] and is beyond the scope of this book, but worth exploring on your next Instant-Gratification-Monkey-driven YouTube binge.

Due dates create a controlled level of stress. They keep the Instant Gratification Monkey from controlling your brain. They keep you acting, moving, progressing, and completing.

IDEA #3: BECOME A PRODUCTIVITY GEEK

Not everyone's wired the same way. Some love to put their head down and get "actual" stuff done. Others love to keep their head in the clouds dreaming of what "could" be done.

---

22   Adam Tarnow, "Stress, The Panic Monster, and You," March 1, 2021, in *Here's What I'm Seeing*, podcast, https://www.audible.com/pd/Stress-The-Panic-Monster-and-You-Podcast/B08XQQB2GK.

Regardless of how you're wired, you have to figure out a way to get stuff done.

Why?

Because talk is cheap. Ideas devoid of a clear path for implementation are basically worthless. Anyone with basic verbal communication skills can talk about what *could* or *should* be done.

What was more impressive about Steve Jobs and the iPhone?

- The idea of an easy-to-use mobile phone, music player, and internet-connected device, or
- The fact that he and the team at Apple developed and shipped the product?

We'd argue it was the latter. He figured out a way to get something done. We're positive that hundreds of other people were also frustrated with the first generation of smartphones and laid awake at night "dreaming" about how it "could" and "should" improve, but Jobs had the tenacity to figure out how to get it done. The accurate marker of success is not the idea—it's the ability to take the idea and develop a product that actually ships to real customers.

Current business culture *loves* to celebrate visionary leaders. As an emerging leader, there's a temptation to listen to all the chatter about vision and believe vision is the essential leadership quality to achieve success.

Don't buy that lie.

Vision is essential, but vision without action is daydreaming. Daydreaming was a fine way to endure a boring class in high school, but it won't move your career or give you an EDGE.

All successful professionals know how to get stuff done. You don't receive a promotion because you come up with good ideas. No, you receive a promotion because you have good ideas, *and* you know how to activate those ideas. So the earlier in your career you start geeking out on getting stuff done, the better.

The more you progress in your career, the higher the probability that you can hire a team around you to do the actual work you don't enjoy doing or are not good at doing. However, you've got to earn that right.

Unless you are the founding owner of the organization you work for, rarely are you immediately given the right just to be an "idea person" and manage the people who do the actual work.

So, for now, be obsessed with getting work done. Don't stop dreaming and ideating. Those are undoubtedly helpful and necessary. But remember, the crowning achievement of Steve Jobs's career was *shipping* the iPhone, not dreaming up the idea.

Raising the value of action in your own life is a great way to stand out by showing you're *all in*.

THE TEDDY ROOSEVELT LIFE HACK

Theodore "Teddy" Roosevelt is known as an American states-man, conservationist, naturalist, historian, and writer, among other things. That's an impressive list of labels. His LinkedIn profile would have looked legit.

Teddy graduated from Harvard, and while attending, he developed a reputation for being one of the hardest working students the university had ever seen. That, too, is an impressive label.

His friends in college said he had "an amazing array of interests."[23] He made plenty of time for boxing, wrestling, bodybuilding, dance lessons, poetry readings, and naturalism, on top of schoolwork. After his freshman year, he published his first book, *The Summer Birds of the Adirondacks*.

At first glance, it might appear that Mr. Roosevelt had an issue with focus. However, upon deeper inspection, what looks like a scattered brain was really a life hack. He discovered a habit that kept him focused on action, movement, progress, and completion.

His secret? Deadlines.

To accomplish all he wanted to accomplish, he would look at his day and block out time on his schedule for each task.

However, he would always give himself *less* time than he thought he needed.

What did this do for him? It awakened the Panic Monster.

Giving himself less time to accomplish what he needed to do (and *wanted* to do) gave him hyper-focus and intensity.

---

23 This whole story is from Cal Newport's *Deep Work: Rules for Focused Success in a Distracted World* (New York: Grand Central Publishing, 2016), 166–167.

Roosevelt's reputation: he had a strong bias toward action.

The result: he quickly made it into the room where it happens. Literally. He was the twenty-sixth president of the United States from September 1901 to March 1909.

Not bad at all for a guy who liked writing about birds and poetry and could kick your butt if you made fun of him because his hobbies included boxing and bodybuilding.

Roosevelt knew that a task always seems to get accomplished in the amount of time you allow.

Be like Teddy. *Talk is cheap, so take action.*

PART 3

GROWTH

**THE HUNGER FOR PROGRESS AND
DEVELOPMENT YOU EMBODY**

CHAPTER 7

SELF-LEADERSHIP

DON'T BE AN OLD DOG—
LEARN A NEW TRICK

Old Spice was started in 1937 by a gentleman named William Lightfoot Schultz.[24] After seventy years, near the end of the aughts, they realized they needed a rebrand. At that time, they were synonymous with just being old. Back then, some brands were considered "cool" for being old, but Old Spice wasn't one. The hipsters had not embraced them like they had adopted Pabst Blue Ribbon.

What did Old Spice do? They ditched the serious old-school approach and adopted a more comical and witty vibe. They created a slew of new products and commercials that were irreverent, yet memorable. They contained shirtless men and even the occasional centaur. Their commercials aired during Super Bowls and included ridiculous banter like this:

---

24 Wikipedia, s.v. "Old Spice," last modified May 18, 2022, 19:53, https://en.wikipedia.org/wiki/Old_Spice.

"Hello, ladies. Look at your man, now back to me, now back at your man, now back to me. Sadly, he isn't me, but if he stopped using ladies scented body wash and switched to Old Spice, he could smell like he's me."

The result? They blew up. Not only did their commercials go viral, but their sales increased. Come to find out, men like to laugh while being body shamed. Who knew?

According to intelligent marketing people, this is one of the most successful rebrands in recent history.[25] Even Adam's young elementary school boys, when given the choice, prefer Old Spice products over Axe, Dove Men+Care, Degree, or Gillette.

Old Spice could have just dug in their heels and said, "Listen, we are who we are. Yes, our target market is primarily men who use hearing aids. Yes, these men all have a bowl of Werther's Original on their coffee table. But listen, without our product, these men would smell like Vick's VapoRub. That's not good. These fine men have gotten us this far, so let's keep selling them average-smelling cologne at a fair price until they pass away. At that point, we will all go find new jobs."

They could have said that, but they didn't. They decided to keep growing. They decided to innovate. They chose to reject the status quo. They decided their brand wasn't fixed; it could evolve, grow, change, mature, and pivot.

---

25   Judith Aquino, "The 10 Most Successful Rebranding Campaigns Ever," *Insider*, February 10, 2011, https://www.businessinsider.com/10-most-successful-rebranding-campaigns-2011-2#there-was-nothing-special-about-old-spice-now-its-a-viral-sensation-8.

They decided to be an old dog who could learn new tricks, and the results speak for themselves.

DISCIPLINE: "HEY OLD SPICE, HOLD MY BEER"

Old Spice crushed its rebranding campaign. Other organizations and businesses have had similar success in reshaping their public image. But one of the most impressive rebranding campaigns we've seen is not a company. It's the rebranding of a word: *discipline.*

In the early 1980s, *discipline* was struggling. No one wanted to pursue a life of *discipline. Discipline* sounded as fun as eating shredded wheat, root canals, jogging, and colonoscopies.

Discipline had a problem, so what did the language gods do? They followed Old Spice's lead. They hired a marketing agency, had a few board meetings, put together some storyboards, drank too many Diet Cokes, and rebranded *discipline* as *self-leadership*! And the tables have turned.

Just Google *self-leadership*, and you'll see what we mean. There are thousands of podcasts, blogs, and books on this subject. It's a success story for the ages!

We like Dr. Charles C. Manz's definition of *self-leadership*: "A process through which individuals control their own behavior, influencing and leading themselves through the use of specific sets of behavioral and cognitive strategies."[26]

---

26   Matteo Cristofaro and Pier Luigi Giardino, "Core Self-Evaluations, Self-Leadership, and the Self-Serving Bias in Managerial Decision Making: A Laboratory Experiment," *Administrative Sciences* 10, no. 3 (September 2020): 64, https://doi.org/10.3390/admsci10030064.

Doesn't that just sound like an overly corporate way to say *discipline*? *Self-leadership* sounds way more important than *discipline*.

THE MOST DIFFICULT PERSON YOU WILL EVER LEAD IS YOU

Whatever you want to call it, self-leadership is a crucial aspect of becoming the professional you desire to be. The reason we say this is because the most difficult person you will ever have to lead is yourself.[27]

Have you ever noticed how gracious and kind you are with yourself? How quickly you give yourself the benefit of the doubt? How often you overrate your general level of awesomeness? How you generally think the world would be a better place if people acted more like you?

This kind of thinking is great for self-esteem, but not so great for development. It's always easier to point out ways other people need to change and grow. That's not impressive. That doesn't set you apart and give you an EDGE.

What's impressive is someone who has a sober view of themselves and humbly understands that if they want to make the world a better place, it starts with them. No, we're not going to quote "Man in the Mirror."

As a human, you are prone to wander. But it's really your brain's fault. As we mentioned in Chapter 5 (Resourcefulness), your brain is wired to conserve energy. In real life, this means, given

---

27 Thank you to Todd Wagner for this idea.

the option, you would prefer to do something nonproductive rather than productive.

This constant temptation to wander is what makes self-leadership so tricky and yet so necessary. As Amor Towles said so well in *A Gentleman in Moscow,* "A man must master his circumstances, or otherwise be mastered by them."

That quote is even better than "Man in the Mirror."

Self-leadership is not an excuse to celebrate "you" and go buy yourself luxurious clothes and fragrances, massages, fine leather goods, and mimosas. It means taking responsibility for your growth. Self-leadership recognizes no one will force you to grow mentally, remain emotionally healthy, improve upon your skills, or set a direction for your future. You have to do it yourself.

In the previous chapter, I mentioned Kobe Bryant's work ethic. One doesn't progress the way he did without self-leadership. His coaches did not show up at his doorstep each morning and make him practice the way he did. Kobe took personal responsibility for his growth. He decided what he would do with his time. He decided when to show up at the gym and when to leave.

Kobe's drive was internal. He called it the Mamba Mentality. Honestly, that's pretty cool to brand your work ethic.

His self-leadership gave him an EDGE, and even if you are not a professional basketball player, you can still learn from his example.

To that end, these three ideas will help you adopt pro-level self-leadership skills.

IDEA #1: RECOGNIZE YOU HAVE ANOTHER JOB TITLE

In 2019, Gallup released the results of their largest global study on the future of work. The number one reason employees change jobs is because they are seeking more "professional or career growth and development opportunities."[28]

Said another way, many aspiring leaders are waiting to be developed, and when it doesn't happen, they leave their job to find what they want.

One of the dirty little secrets of organizational life is that development of employees doesn't happen very often.

In North America, corporate leadership training and development is a $167 billion industry.[29] However, despite this sizeable investment, a study performed by McKinsey & Company determined a large percentage of these dollars are wasted.[30]

Why is there such a disconnect between the investment made and the benefit received? One reason has to do with mindset. Just because someone goes through a formal development program doesn't mean that person *wants* to be developed.

The fact that Corporate America is not very good at developing others is not Corporate America's fault. As the old saying goes, "You can lead a horse to water, but you can't make it drink."

---

28 Jim Clifton and Jim Harter, *It's the Manager* (Washington, DC: Gallup Press, 2019), 99.

29 "Size of the Training Industry," *Training Industry*, last modified March 29, 2021, https://trainingindustry.com/wiki/outsourcing/size-of-training-industry/.

30 Pierre Gurdjian, Thomas Halbeisen, and Kevin Lane, "Why Leadership-Development Programs Fail," *McKinsey Quarterly*, January 1, 2014, https://www.mckinsey.com/featured-insights/leadership/why-leadership-development-programs-fail.

The X factor determining whether an employee develops is the employee's desire and effort, not the number of formal programs offered.

The fact that you are reading this book lets us know you want to develop as a professional. We suggest permanently altering your professional development strategy. Don't rely on employer-sponsored programs as your main source of development. Instead, bring your main source of development "in-house." Embrace your other job title. In addition to your current job title, you are also your own Chief Development Officer.

To be clear, this doesn't mean you reject coaching or other formal training opportunities offered by your employer. What this means is you don't sit around and expect someone else to own your development. You assume your development is your responsibility.

This idea was captured perfectly by Alec Baldwin on an episode of Jerry Seinfeld's *Comedians in Cars Getting Coffee*. Alec joked about the existence of the "Show Business Commission"—an imaginary group that tracks all the underrated talent out there in the world. Once they catch wind of you and your exceptional talent, they come to find you and take you by the hand into the show business industry. He talked about people who are unable to get to the next level and are just hoping the Show Business Commission will show up. He said it's foolish to believe,

"Someone's gonna come and get you and carry you there.

No, they're not."[31]

---

31 *Comedians in Cars Getting Coffee*, created by Jerry Seinfeld, produced by Sony Pictures Television, Embassy Row, and Columbus 81 Productions, 2012, season 10, episode 11.

Those last two sentences are worth rereading: "Someone's gonna come and get you and carry you there...No, they're not."

The quicker you understand this, the faster you'll gain an EDGE and stand out.

You cannot wait for someone to pull you up the corporate ladder. You've got to move toward success yourself. You have to take initiative in this process. You need to develop habits and routines that promote growth. You must understand, in addition to the job title on your business card or LinkedIn profile, you are also your own Chief Development Officer.

You have to take your personal and professional growth personally. How? We're glad you asked. Enter Idea #2.

IDEA #2: WORK THE THREE CATEGORIES

We have found it helpful to think about self-leadership in three categories: head, hands, and heart.

Head: It's Your Responsibility to Continue Learning

Graduating from college is the starting line, not the finish line. Learning never stops until you die. When we say, "learning never stops," we don't say that to sound like the ending of a Hallmark movie.

This is the golden age of learning. It has never been easier to learn—books, podcasts, YouTube, online classes, webinars, conferences, MasterClass, Skillshare. The list is endless.

It boils down to two questions:

1. Do you have the humility to admit there is a lot you still don't know?

2. Will you take the initiative to turn off amusement and turn on learning?

Good self-leadership always involves learning. Take learning seriously, if for no other reason than to look good in meetings.

We cannot tell you how many meetings we've sat in during our careers where one of us "won" the meeting by sharing an idea from the current book we were reading or a podcast episode we had just finished. Truly, it's amazing how many people *don't* keep learning. This is not only the golden age of learning but also the golden age of looking like a genius.

The next time you are on an airplane, look around. It's embarrassing how many adults spend the entire flight playing games on their phones and tablets. These are *adults* playing mindless games! We know we're preaching to the choir, so we hope this encourages you to keep doing what you're doing.

Don't wait for your team leader to give you a book or sign you up for a class. Your education is not your team leader's responsibility. It's yours. The emerging leaders who take responsibility for their learning quickly develop an EDGE.

Ask yourself, *Do I feel like I'm learning and being intellectually challenged?*

Hands: It's Your Responsibility to Keep Acquiring or Honing Skills

"I don't even have any good skills. You know, like nunchuck skills, bowhunting skills, computer hacking skills. Girls only want boyfriends who have great skills!" Napoleon Dynamite had the right mindset to take self-leadership seriously. He had the humility to understand he could get better.

Nunchucks, bowhunting, and computer hacking are not the fast track to promotion (at least, not most of the time), but as we said in Chapter 4 (Competence), professional competence typically is the *quickest* way to get noticed by those already in the room.

Competence builds trust with bosses, peers, and clients. Therefore, pursuing excellence in the core competencies of your profession is a great way to stand out and get noticed.

Say yes to taking on as many new projects or learning as many new technologies as you can. New projects and new technologies often involve learning new skills. Skill accumulation is rarely a bad thing. As David Epstein said so well in his book *Range,* "In most fields—especially those that are complex and unpredictable—generalists, not specialists, are primed to excel."

Again, no one will force you to do this, so it's up to you to adopt the self-leadership mindset and never stop honing or acquiring new skills.

Ask yourself, *Do I feel like I'm getting better and better at my job?*

Heart: It's Your Responsibility to Develop Healthy Habits that Promote Emotional Well-Being

It's no secret. The Trifecta of Well-Being is sleep, diet, and exercise.[32] We touched on this in Chapter 2 (Optimism).

As a leader, you can't just scoff at this and think, *That stuff is for weaklings. I'm different.*

Lack of sleep can lead to long-term irreversible effects. A terrible diet causes you to feel sluggish and uncomfortable. Not exercising makes your body fragile and weak. But for most knowledge workers, the worst part of neglecting the Trifecta of Well-Being isn't the physical impact; it's the emotional impact.

If you doubt what we're saying, just take a few days and visit Disney World. The 2:00 p.m. daily emotional meltdown ain't pretty. The crying. The pouting. The yelling.

Grown men should know how to behave better.

Especially those who have procreated and willingly brought their kids to Disney World.

Life would be easier if it were like a chest of drawers. Wouldn't it be nice if all the various aspects of life were compartmentalized, and one compartment didn't impact another?

- Career
- Family

---

32 For more on this, read *Eat Move Sleep: How Small Choices Lead to Big Changes* (Arlington: Missionday, 2013) by Tom Rath. This is a great entry-level, one-volume resource on this Trifecta of Well-Being.

- Hobby
- Diet
- Exercise
- Money
- Faith
- Friends

Breaking life down into categories looks good on paper. Breaking life down into categories might help you feel like you are in control of life. However, in life, there really is just one category: life, and it is much more complicated and intertwined, like a bowl of spaghetti—nothing like a chest of drawers.

Good self-leadership understands the interconnectedness of life and seeks to develop habits that promote emotional well-being. There is no perfect system. Life is difficult for everyone, and we are all going to have days when we're not at our best emotionally.

There is also no one perfect combination of sleeping, eating, and exercising. Everyone's body is different. We like the way Kim Scott, author of the popular *Radical Candor*, talks about her habits that lead to emotional well-being.

"The world is full of advice here, what is enormously meaningful for one person is pure crap for another...Do whatever works for you...Here's what I need to stay centered: sleep eight hours, exercise for forty-five minutes, and have both breakfast and dinner with my family."[33]

Everyone has a different "recipe." Find yours and stick with it.

---

33 Kim Scott, *Radical Candor: Be a Kickass Boss Without Losing Your Humanity* (New York: St. Martin's Press, 2017).

It's confusing, but Corporate America in general loves to celebrate *neglecting* the Trifecta of Well-Being. It can be a badge of honor to sleep less, never exercise, and eat like trash. "I'll sleep when I'm dead!" Then get ready, because that day is probably coming sooner for you than others!

If the thought of developing three healthy habits that promote emotional well-being is overwhelming to you, then we'd suggest starting with sleep.

If you can start getting a good night's sleep regularly, that will move the needle of well-being faster than eating and exercise and will also give you the emotional resiliency to begin making better food and exercise choices.

So, when in doubt, go to bed.

Ask yourself, *Have I developed good habits that promote emotional well-being?*

IDEA #3: SEEK OUT OPPORTUNITIES TO SAY, "THANKS FOR THE FEEDBACK!"

If you invited us over for dinner, guess what we'd notice the second we walked into your home?

It smells.

Don't worry; we're not judging you. Our homes smell too. Everyone's house has a distinct smell. Scientists call this distinct smell an Occupancy Odor. The crazy thing about your Occupancy Odor is you are the only one who doesn't notice it. No matter how hard you try, you don't recognize your home's Occupancy Odor.

There are differing theories as to why this happens, but most believe it's a biological safety feature. Our brains tune out all familiar smells so we can focus on new or foreign smells.

Things like:

- A trash can that needs emptying
- Something in the refrigerator that's turned sour
- A dirty diaper
- The popcorn burning in the microwave

So what if your Occupancy Odor is unpleasant? How will you ever know so you can fix it?

Feedback.

If you have an unpleasant Occupancy Odor, then you need someone who cares enough to tell you. Otherwise, nothing will change because you don't notice it.

Why do we share all of this?

As a professional, you also have an Occupancy Odor. You have ways of going about your professional life that may not be pleasant.

You have some habits that may need tweaking. Some communication skills that may need sharpening. Some ways of handling stress that might need improvement.

If these "unpleasant smells" go unaddressed, they could prevent you from standing out.

How can you prevent your Professional Occupancy Odor from holding you back? How can you make the necessary tweaks?

Feedback.

A crucial step in your professional journey will be learning to seek out and appreciate feedback. You cannot get better without it. Period.

You need someone (or multiple someones) with the courage to help you see you're not as great as your dog thinks you are.

Feedback, both positive and negative, is crucial in your career journey. No one stands out and gets noticed without feedback. No one.[34]

Here are a few quick thoughts on feedback.

Like most of the principles we've discussed in this chapter, you must seek it out. And, just to be clear, an annual review probably won't be enough. You don't need a rating on a scale of one to five. You need honest answers to questions like these:

A. What skills do I need to develop that would make you comfortable recommending me for a promotion?

---

34   There is so much to say on this topic that is beyond the scope of this book. We highly recommend *Thanks for the Feedback Thanks for the Feedback: The Science and Art of Receiving Feedback Well* (New York: Viking, 2014) by Douglas Stone and Sheila Heen.

B. If I left the organization tomorrow, would the team be better off, worse off, or about the same?
C. Do you trust my competence?
D. Do you trust my character?
E. What makes working with me difficult?
F. What makes working with me pleasant?

The answers to those questions are important and frightening. You need someone in your life who will answer them truthfully, but also compassionately.

Put all feedback into one of two categories: how am I at work? (Sometimes referred to as "hard skills" or "technical skills.") And how am I to work with? (Sometimes referred to as "relational skills" or "soft skills.") Both categories are important, especially if you aspire to one day lead a team.

The skills necessary to get you promoted to a position of leadership are usually technical in nature. Are you a good accountant, architect, teacher, physician, attorney, or business developer? However, once in a position of leadership, the skills necessary to become even more successful are often relational in nature. Are you a good communicator, conflict resolver, developer of people, or vision caster?

Improving technical skills is often different than improving relationship skills. Both are skills you can improve—you just need to approach improvement differently for each, which is why it's helpful to put all feedback in one of these two categories.

The best response to feedback is, "Thank you." Quality feedback (like answers to the questions listed above) is difficult to come by nowadays. We live in an easily offended culture, and few people have the mental resilience to hear anything negative about their life. We believe all people can grow, mature, change, and develop. We assume no one is born as a perfect professional. So if someone is kind enough to share their thoughts with you, just say, "Thank you."

Feedback is a gift that comes with a return receipt. Just because someone gives you feedback doesn't mean you have to absorb and metabolize it. Take the feedback home and try it on. If it doesn't help or doesn't fit, then return it (i.e., ignore it).

We all have a Professional Occupancy Odor. Many times, that odor isn't pleasant. We need people to give us feedback so we can grow and make necessary tweaks. Most successful professionals learn how to make tweaks throughout their careers. It never stops. So the sooner you can start that process, the better.

THE GROWTH MINDSET SHOWS YOU'RE *ALL IN*

In 2006, Carol Dweck, the Lewis and Virginia Eaton Professor of Psychology at Stanford University, published a book titled *Mindset: The New Psychology of Success.* In that book, she detailed the difference between a *growth* mindset and a *fixed* mindset.

According to Dweck, there is a continuum with the fixed mindset on one side and the growth mindset on the other. An individual's place on the fixed mindset and growth mindset continuum is based on their answer to a simple question: "Where does your ability come from?"

Those who believe their success is a result of innate ability are said to have a fixed mindset. If you think that whatever you've achieved up to this point in your life is because you were "born smart" or "came out of your mom's womb with a general propensity for awesomeness," then you have a fixed mindset.

Dweck would argue this mindset is not good for you in the long run.

However, if you believe your success is the result of hard work, learning, training, grit, and tenacity, you are said to have a growth mindset.

Someone with a growth mindset believes their success is a result of hard work. Getting up early, working hard, sweating, going the extra mile, not expecting handouts, and believing you can always get better.

Dweck would argue this mindset is good for you in the long run.

Her research is so popular, even elementary school students are being taught the difference between a growth mindset and a fixed mindset. This is a good thing.

We close with this because self-leadership and a growth mindset go hand in hand. They are two sides of the same coin. You can't have one without the other.

Self-leadership rejects the status quo. It accepts responsibility. Self-leadership will give you an EDGE and cause you to stand out by showing you're *all in*. Don't wait for the Show Business Commission to show up and take you somewhere. Embrace your new job title, never stop learning, seek out new skills, develop healthy habits, and request feedback. Do these, and your career will be anything but fixed.

CHAPTER 8

OWNERSHIP

BOSSES SAY THE DARNDEST THINGS

Being a team leader and a boss is hard work. It really is. The responsibility, the decisions, the pressure, the accountability, and the expectations can all add up. The relentless burden of leading others, in our minds, justifies a leader's higher pay. Leading and serving people is not glamorous work. Yes, at times it can be extremely satisfying and fun, but most of the time it's just hard work.

We say all that to butter-up team leaders and bosses because we're about to make fun of them.

In addition to all the buzz words discussed in Chapter 4 (Competence), why do team leaders and bosses have so many strange phrases? Do they all go to boss school and learn the same phrases and isms?

In addition to the regular phrases like, "hit the ground running," "thinking outside the box," and "discussing offline," team leaders and bosses can also say some really mean and (potentially) hurtful things too.

In October 2014, *Inc. Magazine* published a list of 49 dumb things bosses said.[35] Geoffrey James, the author of the list, had been collecting "management gems" for years. Every time he heard about a horrible thing a boss said, he wrote it down. For obvious copyright reasons, I won't publish the entire list, but I do want to share my top five:

1. "I know that I am a great leader. This department, however, needs help learning to follow."

2. "I never micromanage, but I do need to know everything that's going on."

3. "I'm sorry if I ever gave you the impression your input would have any effect on my final decision."

4. "Our efforts to expand overseas are hampered because they don't speak English."

5. "It has come to my attention that your salary is well below the industry average. Therefore, I am changing your title."

When we read the list, we didn't know if we should laugh or cry. Maybe we watched a few too many episodes of *The Office* during quarantine, but it's not hard to picture a boss somewhere in the world making those statements.

---

35   Geoffrey James, ed., "49 Dumb Things Bosses Really Said," *Inc.*, October 10, 2014, https://www.inc.com/geoffrey-james/49-dumb-things-bosses-really-said.html

In the end, we put most boss-speak in the same category as dad jokes. Annoying? For sure. Mean or hurtful? Rarely.

MY LEAST FAVORITE BOSS QUOTE

Whenever a boss or team leader says anything about "ownership," my eyes involuntarily roll. I don't know why, but team leaders and business owners *love* to encourage their teams to "act like an owner," "take ownership," and "own this idea like it's your idea."

If you haven't heard it yet, just wait.

When I was a young leader and ran into the admonition to "act like an owner," I remember instantly disliking it.

At the time, I was working twelve- to fourteen-hour days. I was constantly in touch with my team, even when not at work. I had a customer-facing job, so there was a sense of impending doom hovering over my existence at all times. I felt like I was always working.

I had a constant nagging feeling that at any moment, I could get a call about a frustrated customer or a transaction that fell apart. Work was the air I breathed. Said another way: I was working hard, and I was working a lot.

I was doing everything I could to keep a team, grow a team, and really, just survive.

So when I was told, "Hey, David, act like an owner," my first thought was, *Isn't that what I'm doing? I mean, I'm working my tail off and making it happen every day. How about this?*

How about instead of telling me to "act like an owner," why don't you start paying me like one!

Don't worry. I didn't say that. You shouldn't either. That's a whole different leadership lesson: *The things we think and do not say.*[36]

Back to the point.

If we're honest with ourselves, we have some snarkiness in our hard-working and ambitious souls. When someone with a larger paycheck, more autonomy, and what appears to us like a pretty darn good day-to-day life tells us to "act like an owner," we recoil and get defensive.

However, buried in this statement is a clue. When team leaders and bosses say this, they are really being assertive and vulnerable. They are making it clear how to stand out by showing you're *all in.*

Bosses and team leaders only say these words when they feel like the team could be showing more effort, more desire, or more aspiration. They also say these words if they feel like the team is acting too siloed and not seeing the big picture.

PRACTICE YOUR JUDO: THINK DON'T ACT

I'm not a martial arts expert, but I've seen all of *The Karate Kid* films. Yes, even the one with Hilary Swank. No, it was not very good.

---

36 The phrase above is also the title of a famous memo written by Jerry Maguire, played by Tom Cruise, in the 1996 movie of the same name.

There are numerous types of martial arts, but the most interesting one to me is Judo. Judo is the Jedi Mind Trick of martial arts. Judo is not about attacking as much as it is about using your opponent's strength and momentum against themselves.

Judo (Japanese for "the gentle way") emphasizes winning in combat by using your opponent's weight and strength as weapons against him while preserving your own mental and physical energy. It embodies the principle that good technique can win out over sheer strength.[37]

Rather than take the phrase "act like an owner" and simply place it on a list of annoying boss-speak, take a moment and see how you can use it to your advantage. Use some good techniques to gain an EDGE.

Acting like an owner might feel inauthentic. Most people (other than actors) don't come to work each day to "act." They come to work each day to "work."

The first Judo move is to reframe the way you interpret the phrase, "act like an owner." Substitute the word "act" for the word "think." Learning to *think like the owner* is more authentic than trying to *act like an owner*. We know this is subtle, but we believe it's important and even more helpful.

Owners act differently because they think differently. If you can learn to think like an owner now, you will be a better team leader (and owner) later. It's like you're in ownership training.

---

37 Jill Rosenfeld, "The Art of Business Judo," Fast Company, July 31, 2001, https://www.fastcompany.com/43353/art-business-judo#:~:text=Judo%20(Japanese%20for%20%E2%80%9Cthe%20gentle,win%20out%20over%20sheer%20strength.

You get to make all the mistakes while the mistakes don't cost people their jobs.

Take the opportunity to learn how owners *think* before you have to pay ownership prices for faulty thinking.

You might be wondering, what do owners think about? Do they think about how awesome it is to be rich? How difficult it is to find a quality yacht at a good price? How fun it is to drive nice cars? Hardly.

The two most common things an owner thinks about are cash flow and the future.

CASH FLOW

The simple truth is this: your organization needs cash to survive.

Drilling down a little further: specifically, owners think about how the organization can generate positive cash flow. How they can make sure more cash comes *into* the organization than goes *out* of the organization.

This is why owners are obsessed with sales and costs. Nobody gets paid without positive cash flow, and no one gets a bonus without positive cash flow (and profit).

Your organization needs cash, and the owner wants it to all work. The salaries, the bonus structures, the benefits, the product, the customer satisfaction. All of it.

Most bosses and team leaders agree with venture capitalist Frederick Adler when he says, "Happiness is positive cash flow."

THE FUTURE

Much of an owner's job is living in the future. Spotting trends, looking for patterns, and trying to determine what's coming next to your market or industry.

Why do they think about this stuff? They want to make sure the organization is ready to take on new challenges and maintain the ability to generate positive cash flow.

Owners are, at minimum, living three months ahead of everyone else, but may be as much as a full twelve months ahead.

Jeff Bezos once said, "I don't need anyone reporting to me who is worried about the quarterly numbers." We can guarantee he wants his quarterly numbers to go up and to the right (that's why he needs you, by the way). So why would he say he doesn't want anyone on his team worried about that?

Because he's thinking about the long-term future, not just the next quarter. Bezos has the privilege of both thinking *and* acting like an owner. Owners are thinking strategically, not tactically. They live in and are ever mindful of the future.

SNAP BACK TO REALITY, OH THERE GOES GRAVITY

Before we get to the third way for you to begin thinking more like an owner, we want to throw in one more freebie. Since many owners are thinking and living in the future, you can help them by doing the opposite. Especially if the owner of your organization isn't involved in the day-to-day details of the operation.

Confused? Let us explain.

If you work for an owner who is not involved in the everyday details, take any opportunity you can to let them know how things are *really* going. Sometimes, when an owner is not involved in the day-to-day, they can lose touch with reality. They can build up in their minds how the operation is functioning, and sometimes those figments of their imagination are not true. They need you to help them keep the pulse on reality.

I once took a job with a new company. I was good friends with the owner. Although we were friends, we were nowhere near each other on the organizational chart. He was on top. I was not.

We'd get together on occasion for social events, and work would always become the topic of conversation. In those short little conversations, I can remember saying several times (with as much tact as possible), "That's actually not how it goes down," or "This might sound strange to you, but no one really does it that way."

His response was always some combination of annoyance, shock, and appreciation for an honest look at the business. I always made sure to end the conversation with some notes on things that were going well in the organization.

Now, fair warning: if you try this, you're treading on thin ice. You can't just burst into the CEO's office and yell, "You sit on a throne of lies!" Don't do that.

I'm not suggesting you act like a detective and then share the evidence with the boss. I'm not suggesting you dump trash on the boss's desk. (Remember Chapter 5?) I'm suggesting you think as you work. Be ready to give insight when it's requested.

Think about how things are supposed to go. Was this the plan? How is the reality of your operation deviating from the initial strategy? How can this project be better? Think. Think. Think. Don't speak.

Invariably, the moment will come when you will have the opportunity to speak, and then you'll be ready to provide helpful insight. (More on this later.)

So, with all that being said, here are three ideas to help you think differently—ideas to help you *think* like an owner.

IDEA #1: STUDY UP ON THE BASIC ECONOMICS OF YOUR ORGANIZATION

As we just mentioned above, most owners think about cash flow. Therefore, understanding the basic economics of your organization helps you stand out.

Detailed financial information may not be easy to access for nonexecutive leaders, but that's okay. You don't need to know as much as your organization's chief financial officer. Start with trying to answer a few basic questions:

- How is revenue generated?
- What are the highest costs?
- Which product or service is the most profitable?
- Is cash flow consistent throughout the year or seasonal?
- How does your specific job impact profitability? (Are you a cost-center or a revenue producer?)

I worked for a time in food service. In that business, there are two considerable costs: food and labor. That's it. If you control food and labor, you win. A third area of focus is repairs and maintenance. It's not as big as food and labor, but you have to be mindful of it, or a molehill will become a mountain, and you'll get in trouble.

In the food service world, the whole game is to grow sales, control food and labor costs, and be mindful of repairs and maintenance expenses. Do that week-to-week and month-to-month, and you've got yourself a nice little profit.

Every industry or company has a similar structure. The faster you understand the basic economics of your organization (and industry), the faster you gain an EDGE.

IDEA #2: FOCUS ON THE NUMBERS THAT MATTER MOST TO THE CURRENT OWNERS

Cleanliness is a big deal in the restaurant business. This is not news. You don't have to be in food service to know that everyone prefers a clean and tidy restaurant.

But here's a funny thing about running restaurants. Every boss has their cleanliness pet peeve.

I had a boss once who judged you on the threshold of the door. If the threshold was dirty, he didn't care about the rest. I didn't even know what a threshold was until I worked for this boss.

Another boss judged me by the legs of the equipment. The legs! To be clear, we made exactly zero food on the legs, but it didn't matter to this boss. If the counter legs or table legs were grimy, done. I failed.

I could go on and on. Suffice to say, each boss nitpicked a different thing.

To succeed in my organization, I had to care about cleanliness, in general, but specifically the areas my boss cared about. I cared about the cleanliness of the kitchen, the threshold, the bathroom, and the dining room. However, I *really* cared about the legs of the table. That's how I made sure to stand out with my boss.

So what is the thing your boss cares about? Customer numbers? Referrals? The number of calls attempted? Net promoter score? Social media engagement?

My encouragement to you is this: focus on what your boss cares about. What goal is she pursuing? What is her current obsession? And why? How can you help her achieve that goal, make that sale, hit that target?

The chances are high that your team leader is pretty intelligent. If she has a company big enough to employ more than two people, then she's smart. And nobody knows the ins and outs of her business better than she does.

When you learn from her and begin to care about the numbers she cares about, that lets her know you're *all in*.

IDEA #3: REGULARLY ASK YOURSELF, "HOW DO I IMPACT
_____?"

How do you fill in the blank? With whatever key metrics you learned as you *focused on the numbers that matter most* to your boss (Idea #2).

Employees generally think like this:

- *How am I impacted by leadership's decisions?*
- *Will this new sales initiative give me more work?*
- *Will this reorganization put me on a team I don't like?*
- *Will this new cost-cutting measure make my job more difficult?*
- *If we merge with this other company, does that mean I'll have to learn a whole new accounting system?*

To stand out, think differently.

After you understand the basic economics of your organization and what your team leader cares about, start to see the role you play in impacting those numbers. Think about how your actions impact others and your company as a whole. This is a game-changer, and it will cause you to stand out.

Owners think about how ideas impact the bottom line, the employees, the market, the board of directors, the community in which they serve or do business, and the list goes on. Owners think about the holistic and large-scale impact of decisions and ideas.

We suggest you start thinking this way too.

We're assuming your owner is a decent human. However, we're not naive. We realize plenty of owners don't act in the best interest of their employees, community, or the environment. But we assume when you are responsible for leading a large team, you'll be motivated to do it the right way. So let's keep assuming we're all good people here.

And to that point. It doesn't suddenly get easy to consider the needs of others or the environment when you gain a leadership title. You don't undergo some kind of Captain America–type transformation when that day arrives.

If you are self-interested and me-focused before the invitation, you'll probably be that way when you're part of the decision-making team. Don't wait for the magic Hollywood moment where you go from a self-interested employee to a generous boss.

You *are* what you are *becoming*.

Start now. Start thinking like a good boss, like a good owner. Start thinking like the owner you wish you had or, hopefully, the owner you do have.

Start considering others' needs. Start thinking of the larger impact of a decision. Here are some questions to ask yourself:

- What does our board need/want from us this year or quarter?
- How are we perceived in the community, and how can we be better?
- What is the bottom line, and how are we strategically going to improve it?
- What's the purpose of my division? What's *the ultimate win* for all stakeholders?
- What is my boss's biggest need? Why does he need it?

Ask those questions, and you can authentically say you are learning to think like the owner without needing to act like anyone other than yourself.

LEARN FROM DWIGHT

After working with various bosses and team leaders over the years, there is one thing that has become clear: most bosses and team leaders don't *really* want every employee to "act like an owner."

Think about how chaotic it would be if each employee at your company acted like an owner. Everyone would be stepping on toes, questioning the board's decisions, giving input where you're not invited to do so, etc. Nothing would get done.

You may be familiar with an example of what acting like an owner can do if handled incorrectly. You become Dwight from *The Office*, and you'll just be the person in the workplace everyone laughs at (not with) because you live in a dream world where you think you're the "Assistant Branch Manager," but in reality, you're just an "Assistant *to the* Branch Manager," which, for the record, wasn't even really a thing.

Get the point?

There is a sizable difference between *thinking* like an owner and *acting* like one.

When you *think* like an owner, you get all the benefits of preparation and none of the liability of assumption.

When the boss asks for input randomly, you're ready. Because you've been thinking like an owner for a long time. When you add value in those seemingly random moments, you'll begin to notice the boss coming to you more frequently.

I recently went to a location to visit the employees. I walked up to one of our great managers and asked how long he had been with us (three years). After learning he had previously worked for our competitor, I said, "Tell me one thing our competitor does well that we don't do here." He replied: "Man, that's a great question. I don't know."

Fail.

If he had been thinking like an owner for the past three years, he would have had an insightful and likely passionate answer. He didn't because he wasn't.

And that's a big deal.

Think like an owner.

When you learn to think like the owner, you can't help but stand out. That level of *all in* is rare. Not many people are seeking to think like an owner, which is why you have such a prime opportunity to take control of your career.

CHAPTER 9

FLEXIBILITY

A PASTOR WHO CUSSES
AND A CURVEBALL

Jim Wimberley served on staff at Watermark Community Church in Dallas, Texas, for almost twenty years. Jim was beloved by everyone on the team, and the day he retired was a sad day. If you met Jim, you would notice three things:

1. He's funny. He loves to laugh, and his favorite joke target is himself (especially his age—Jim is in his eighties).

2. He prays a lot. He is one of those rare people who writes stuff down and then actually prays for you. In fact, he and his wife are known for taking "prayer walks" multiple times a week. We need more people like Jim in the world.

3. He's known to have a bit of a foul mouth, though it's occasional and nothing major. If Jim's life were a movie, it would be rated PG.

Two of his favorite sayings are fart-face and sissy. You know, things any grown man in his eighties says regularly. But Jim's most famous foul-mouthed saying is, "If it's not one damn thing, it's another damn thing."

What we find funny about Jim's "damn" statement is that it's not meant to be funny. It's meant to serve as a reminder that life doesn't always work out the way you want it to.

If "Life" were a major league baseball pitcher, it would be in the Hall of Fame as one of the nastiest and most successful pitchers ever. Life's go-to strike-out pitch, without a doubt, is the curve-ball—a pitch Life throws our way all the time.

THAT DAMN STATEMENT IS THE TRUTH

The more we think about Jim's damn statement, the more we see how helpful it is. Especially for aspiring leaders.

Jim's statement confronts one of the most disturbing realities of leadership—uncertainty.

For every leader on the planet, the future is uncertain. It cannot be relied on. It cannot be known. It is not definite.

This doesn't mean the future is always doom and gloom. However, it does mean that the future is always fuzzy and, therefore, a bit stressful.

This section discusses how the hunger for progress and effort—growth—will set you apart. Growth is seen in self-leadership

(Chapter 7), thinking like an owner (Chapter 8), and remaining flexible when dealing with uncertainty (this chapter).

No leader ever knows what damn thing life is going to throw their way tomorrow. As an emerging leader, when you choose flexibility over frustration in the face of uncertainty, you are letting everyone know you're *all in.*

Facing uncertainty head-on is one of the fastest ways to grow as a leader because uncertainty is a constant reality. The sooner you get comfortable with it, the better it will be for you and the team you lead.

Below are three ideas that will help you deal with the next damn thing life throws your way.

IDEA #1: GET COMFORTABLE SAYING, "I DON'T KNOW, BUT I'LL FIND OUT"

Unexpected news, unforeseen circumstances, unexpected results. Leaders deal with curveballs all the time. If life didn't throw us curveballs, there would be no need for a leader. Curveballs give leaders job security.

"The client didn't get us the information on time. Now we're delayed. What should we do?"

"There was a flaw in the manufacturing process. The entire batch is ruined. Again. What now?"

"Sarah and Davey both turned in their two-week notice. What do we tell the client? We promised we'd put them on this project."

"The local officials just said everyone has to stay home for at least six weeks. What about this conference we've been planning for the last six months?"

As a leader, you can't escape uncertainty. It's perpetual and never-ending. You are the batter, and *Life* is the pitcher. The manager never takes Life out of the game. Curveball after curveball will never stop coming your way.

So when Life throws you one of its nasty curveballs, how you respond matters. The way we see it, you have two options:

1. Pretend you know exactly what to do, even when you don't.

2. Be honest.

We suggest option number two.

You're thinking, *But if I'm honest, what will that do to team morale? That won't instill any confidence.*

We understand that line of thinking, but we still believe honesty is better than lying. Always. There is a big difference between confidently saying, "I don't know, but I'll find out," and hesitantly talking in circles, making it obvious to everyone that you have no clue what you're saying.

Pretending to know when you don't is a sign of insecurity, not a sign of good leadership.[38] Giving an answer when it's clear you don't have one is a sign of insecurity, not maturity. Insecurity

---

[38] Andy Stanley, *Next Generation Leader: Five Essentials for Those Who Will Shape the Future* (Colorado Springs: Multnomah Books, 2003), 94.

is one of those issues that is visible to everyone else long before it's visible to you. Unfortunately, with insecurity, you're the last to know. And as a leader, that's never a good thing.[39]

Again, we understand the desire to give confident answers when uncertainty arises, but in the end, if you are not confident in your answer, it's best to simply say, "I don't know, but I'll find out."

As an emerging leader, practicing your response to uncertainty helps solidify your reputation. Resisting the urge to pretend you know when you don't builds trust.

Saying "I don't know, but I'll find out" with confidence doesn't erode trust, it builds it.

Saying "I don't know, but I'll find out" communicates to your team and team leader that you are not giving up or abdicating your responsibility.

It shows that you are flexible and willing to pivot when uncertainty comes your way.

It communicates that you are not expecting someone else to do the work you need to do. It's an honest answer and the best response to Life's nasty curveballs.

Eliminate as Many Surprises as You Can

Life's curveballs typically show up as a surprise. Even though

---

39 You may recall the children's story about the Emperor and his new clothes.

we all know surprises happen, when they do, it's not always a good thing.

Want to gain some extra attention from your team leader or boss? Do what you can to eliminate the number of surprises they experience throughout the day. Your surprise doesn't have to also be your boss's surprise.

Sometimes a surprise isn't actually a result of uncertainty but a result of poor communication. Doing what you can to improve communication can eliminate the number of surprises your team leader faces each day.

You might be thinking, *What? Doesn't everyone love a good surprise?*

The answer is a resounding, "No!" Our cussing pastor friend might say, "Hell no!"

If you can develop a reputation as the person who eliminates surprises, then you'll quickly become a trusted member of the team.

Did you come across some information you believe your team leader will appreciate? Share it.

Uncover a mistake that was made by your team? Make sure the team leader knows as soon as possible!

Play out this scenario in your mind: if your team leader were sitting in a meeting, and his boss said to him, "Did you know _____ happened?" you want him to be able to say, "Yes, I did know. In fact, it's next on my list to discuss with you.

I'm aware it happened, and my team has already come up with three different ways to make sure this doesn't happen again."

Arming your team leader with that kind of intelligence is a win for everyone and will cause you to stand out faster than a Formula 1 driver flies around a racetrack.

IDEA #2: DEVELOP THE HABIT OF SEEKING COUNSEL

Solomon, the ancient king of Israel, once said, "Get all the advice and instruction you can, so you will be wise the rest of your life."[40]

Why do we share this pithy axiom from a dead king? Because one of the best habits to develop in the face of uncertainty is tapping into your personal network for advice and counsel.

If you are facing a situation you've never faced before, it doesn't make much sense to "go rogue" and try to figure it out on your own. It makes much more sense to tap into the collective wisdom of others.

This is much easier said than done because so many people believe being a great leader means you must have all the answers to all the problems. Nothing could be further from the truth.

The prerequisite for leadership is not book smarts, it's humility. One of the reasons a humble leader is a great leader is because they are humble enough and flexible enough to seek counsel when facing uncertainty and difficult decisions.

---

40 Proverbs 19:20 (New Living Translation).

If the future is blurry and unknown, how will another person's perspective help me?

Isn't seeking counsel just the blind leading the blind?

We can certainly understand why you would ask these questions. Sometimes, the uncertainty you face is only uncertain to you because you're facing it for the first time.

Of course, there are things like global pandemics that take everyone by surprise—moments of universal uncertainty. But in most cases, our personal uncertainty is someone else's past experience.

Also, seeking counsel is more about the process than the result. When you ask other people their perspective on a situation you're facing, they may not give you the answer, but they can give you new ways to think about it.

Leaders facing uncertainty have an opportunity to use their creativity. The creative process is rarely linear. Jonathan Pokluda, a friend, used to say, "Bad ideas lead to good ideas." That's the creative process in a nutshell.

So when you seek counsel, you might not get the exact answer, but someone else's idea might spark an idea in you that leads to the right answer.

But isn't seeking counsel passing my hard work off on someone else? Didn't you tell me in Chapter 5 (Resourcefulness) to be a problem solver and not dump my trash on someone's desk?

No, seeking counsel is not passing off your hard work onto someone else. It's simply engaging in a conversation with someone to learn and gain new perspectives. When we're facing difficult circumstances, we don't say, "Hey, I've got a thorny problem I'm trying to solve, but I don't want to. Will you kindly solve it for me?"

Typically, we say something like, "Hey, I've got a thorny problem I'm trying to solve. I'd love to get your thoughts on the matter. Can I get ten minutes of your time?" Or, "Can I pick your brain on a situation I'm facing? I think your experience will be helpful."

The thing about seeking counsel is this: when you reach out to someone seeking their advice, it's a compliment to them, and it makes them feel special. Typically, people have no trouble finding time on their calendar for brain-picking or perspective-seeking.

Yes, in Chapter 5, we did tell you to not pass your problems off to someone else. Again, seeking counsel doesn't show an abdication of responsibility, it shows you care. That's why seeking counsel is another way to stand out by showing you're *all in*.

Imagine a scenario where you have to discuss a "curveball" with your team leader. You start out, "Abbey, as you know, the labor shortage is putting a lot of stress on the team. I have never faced this situation before, nor has the company. We have no clue what the future holds and whether or not this situation is going to be resolved in the next ninety days or the next ninety months. So, here's what I did..."

Which one do you think will sound better to your team leader?

1. I drank three bourbons and then began to do the *New York*

Times crossword puzzle. Of course, it was the Monday edition, because that's the easiest one of the week, and after three bourbons, I needed something easy. Now, as you know, I'm not necessarily a believer in astrology, but I do believe the universe talks to me through the *New York Times* crossword puzzle. So, as I was doing the puzzle, there was one clue that helped me figure out how to solve this labor shortage problem. The clue read "Bring to an end," and the answer had five letters. The answer was "cease." So, right then and there, I knew I had the answer. How are we going to respond to the labor shortage? Easy: we're shutting down the entire company. Labor shortage, labor smortage! If we can't beat them, we'll join them. They don't want our jobs? Fine, we'll go take their jobs.

2. I discussed the issue with three other leaders. I have friends at Company X and Company Y. They were immensely helpful. Based on what they are hearing, they think this issue will last at least another twelve months. So, they are preparing to do three things over the next twelve months. I don't think all three of them are helpful for our situation, but I do think one of them is worth considering. Would you like to hear more?

Which one of those sounds like you are more committed to the company and the mission? Which one sounds more thoughtful? Correct—the second one.

So one of the best ways to deal with uncertainty is to get in the habit of seeking counsel. That level of resourcefulness helps you grow, communicates that you care, keeps you humble, and gives you better ideas and solutions for dealing with the thorny problems you will constantly face as a leader.

IDEA #3: LEARN THE ART OF CONSTANT READJUSTMENT

Can you imagine how difficult it is to be the director of a news program or the editor at a newspaper?

You plan and prepare a great late local news show or a helpful issue of the paper and then, one hour before airtime or one hour before you hit "print," the president holds a news conference or a tragic event happens in some part of the world.

At that moment, all your hard work is thrown out the window and you scramble to change your program flow or headlines.

They must think, *You know what really bothers me about this job? All the breaking news! It's so annoying. Why do big things have to happen forty-five minutes before we go live? Can't they wait until the evening newscast is over? Sheesh. They are so selfish!*

To survive in the news industry, you must choose to adapt when things change. Why? Because things change all the time, and if you don't adapt, then you'll just be frustrated all the time! Who wants that?

What's true in the news industry is true in every industry. The ability to adapt is one of the best ways to embrace uncertainty and the inevitable changes that uncertainty brings.

Abbott Laboratories used to have a mantra: "Planning is priceless, but plans are useless."[41] Those are words to live by.

---

41 Jim Collins, *Good to Great: Why Some Companies Make the Leap and Others* Don't (New York: Harper Business, 2001), 123.

The act of planning and thinking about your preferred future is a priceless exercise. We've mentioned this already, but thoughtfulness is rare nowadays. However, plans themselves rarely happen as planned. So when your priceless plans are prevented due to uncertainty, it's time to be flexible. It's time to pivot. As you'll see, pivots, not plans, make you a legendary leader.

In our culture, military leaders are heroes, as they should be. Douglas MacArthur, Colin Powell, Stanley McChrystal, Norman Schwarzkopf, and George Patton are well known for good reason. They served their country with courage and deserve to have their names forever etched in our minds.

We're lucky to have some dear friends who served in the military, and these friends have taught us much about leadership (and life).

Nathan Wagnon, a friend, was a captain in the Army and did two tours in Afghanistan. He uses a common military phrase: "The enemy gets a vote." This means that the best battle plans are just that: plans. In the military, you never assume the enemy will accept your rules of war and abide by them. You must remain flexible—otherwise, you'll lose.

Excellent military leaders do not become legends because of their perfectly executed plans; they become legends because of their ability to pivot when the enemy starts to vote. They choose to be flexible, not frustrated.

When things begin to go differently than you planned, you must learn how to switch your plans. You must learn how to "pivot."

You, too, must learn how to be adaptable, not frustrated, when there is a change of plans.

The ability to pivot is what makes a military leader truly successful. When the enemy starts to vote, strong leaders make the right changes at the right time.

Learning to do this and not get mad about it is an essential leadership skill. "Innovate or die" is a popular leadership axiom because successful leaders have learned the hard way that if you don't learn to pivot when the enemy starts to vote, you will not make it.

Don't believe us? Revisit Chapter 4 (Competence) and the story of Blockbuster Video. As the market started to change its movie-viewing habits, Blockbuster stuck with the plan. Now it's an answer in Tuesday Night trivia games in bars across the nation, not a trusted home entertainment brand.

MISSION OVER METHODS

You might be thinking, *Doesn't all this changing of plans make you fickle?* Shouldn't organizations be more disciplined and ride out a few storms before making changes?

Great questions.

Healthy organizations that adapt to change understand the difference between their mission and their methods. Successful organizations are married to their mission and are just friends with their methods.

Here's a simple example: a local food bank.

The food bank in your area has a mission. Its mission is to feed the under-resourced in the community. They are married to that mission.

Their main method for serving the under-resourced in the community might be to keep a physical space where people can come obtain the food they need.

Their primary method for generating donations might be to host various fundraisers throughout the year. A golf tournament in the spring, a silent auction in the fall, a casino-inspired party on New Year's Eve.

If the food bank is a healthy organization, then it will be staunchly married to its *mission* (feeding the under-resourced in the community), and it will be just friends with its *methods*.

Hopefully, the marriage to the mission will last a long, long time, and they can serve thousands of families. Hopefully, they won't get drunk one night, download a dating app, meet someone else, divorce their original mission, and decide to open a vegan-inspired, high-end grocery store. Not that there is anything wrong with that type of grocery store, but you get what we mean.

The *methods*, however, can (and probably will) change over time. The food bank may offer new ways to obtain food. They might offer home delivery or open new locations. They may come up with new ways to generate donations, like promoting online donations instead of hosting the annual golf tournament.

This is what healthy organizations do. So if you work for a healthy organization, get ready for change, and embrace it when it shows up. Healthy organizations have a culture of flexibility, not a culture of frustration.

Yes, this might mean you can't plan out every detail about your life.

Yes, this might mean something can change at any moment, so you can never fully rest, but that's okay. You will build endurance, which we'll discuss further in the next chapter.

ALWAYS ANOTHER DAMN THING

One of the few guarantees in leadership is uncertainty. As Andy Stanley says, "It's a permanent part of the leadership landscape, and it increases with increased responsibility."

Said another way, there will always be another damn thing headed your way. This is not cause for discouragement or depression—it is cause for leadership. If life were filled with absolute certainty, no one would need a leader.

If you are reading this book, it means you were alive during the pandemic. The pandemic was (and at the time of writing, still is) a big damn thing. It taught us all to choose flexibility over frustration, and it served as a reminder that it is possible to navigate uncertainty.

When the pandemic ends, we cannot for one moment believe uncertainty will also end. It won't.

The habits you developed during this season need to stay with you forever. Don't pretend to know what the future will bring when you don't. Say, "I don't know, but I'll find out."

Continue to develop the habit of seeking counsel in the face of uncertainty. You never know what insight or perspective will lead you to the best solution for you and your team.

And most of all, learn the art of constant readjustment.

If you can begin to grow in the face of uncertainty, you will quickly stand out. The typical reaction to uncertainty is complaining, whining, and bad moods. Don't be common. If you want to communicate something different to your team leader, choose to remain flexible in the face of uncertainty.

RESILIENCE

PEACEMAKER

ENDURANCE

PATIENCE

PART 4

ENDURANCE

THE CHARACTER YOU DEMONSTRATE IN THE FACE OF DIFFICULTY

CHAPTER 10

RESILIENCE

ONE NANOSECOND EQUALS TEN THOUSAND HOURS

It was 5:30 a.m. on November 15, 2019, when Ryan Martin was dropped off on the side of a mountain in Craig, Colorado. All he had with him were the clothes on his back, a water bottle, and a .270 caliber hunting rifle. It was pitch black and eleven degrees.

Ryan was hunting elk. He knew he was in the right spot, so he waited...for hours. Ryan is an experienced hunter, so when he saw an elk, he knew exactly what to do. He looked through the scope and waited quietly for his shot as the adrenaline started to rush through his body.

Unfortunately, the elk that appeared in his crosshairs was a female, and his permit was for a male.

He stood up to catch his breath and reposition. It's not uncommon for male elk to follow behind females as they migrate through the mountain forest.

The terrain on the side of the mountain was rugged (he was in the Rockies, after all). As he started seeking a better spot, he took a step and lost his footing. As he slipped, he felt the rifle slide out of his hands, and his instincts took over—he reached for it so it wouldn't hit the ground and discharge.

That's when his thumb accidentally engaged the trigger. At point-blank range, Ryan shot a .270 caliber bullet through his left leg, just above his ankle.

Ryan is a trained medical professional, but until that morning, he never had to use his skills on himself. The first ten minutes after the accident was pure shock and panic. His ears were ringing, and he couldn't stop saying to himself, "I just shot my leg. I just shot my leg."

Once he started thinking more clearly and his survival instincts and medical training kicked in, he focused on getting to the rendezvous point to meet his friends by any means possible, which included crab-crawling, sliding inch-by-inch up the mountain, leaving a trail of blood behind.

His friends eventually found him, and after multiple hospitals, doctors, and surgeries, all of which were instrumental in saving his life, Ryan returned home to Dallas, and reality finally set in. This injury was significant. He was not going to recover in a week or two. It was after he got home that he realized climbing up a mountain on his back was nothing compared to the mountain of recovery he had ahead of him.

Fast forward to today. As we write this, it's been twenty-four months since Ryan's injury, and he has been through eight surgeries, he's missed approximately forty days of work, he has four permanent pieces of hardware in his leg, and he wasn't able to walk for fourteen months.

It took him a nanosecond to accidentally pull the trigger and injure his leg. It took him over ten thousand hours to walk again.

What enables someone to endure that kind of recovery?

One word: resilience.

Resilience is "(1) the capability of a strained body to recover its size and shape after deformation caused especially by compressive stress and (2) an ability to recover from or adjust easily to misfortune or change."[42]

This word perfectly describes Ryan Martin's body and his character.

This is also a word that needs to describe you if you have hopes for a successful and enduring career.

THE REPUTATION YOU DON'T WANT TO EARN

Resilience is not a word used too often in organizational life. Organizations don't like to describe themselves as "resilient." They prefer words like agile, fast-paced, successful, and dynamic. Resilience implies hardship and failure. That's why most organizations shy away from it.

---

42 *Merriam-Webster*, s.v. "resilience," accessed June 22, 2021, https://www.merriam-webster.com/dictionary/resilience.

The same can be said of you as an emerging leader. You probably don't want to earn the reputation of being resilient. It's not that you would get angry if someone called you resilient, but few people want to go through the hard work of developing this characteristic.

Why? Because, as we said above, developing resilience involves hardship.

Resilience is one of those character traits that can only be shown *after* experiencing something difficult. You don't show anyone how tough you are until you face difficult circumstances. You don't prove you can bounce back until you've been knocked down. Resilience is difficult to display when everything is going perfectly.

STAY, FORREST! STAY!

In 1994, the movie *Forrest Gump* was released and became a smash hit, earning close to $700 million worldwide at the box office and winning six Oscars, including Best Picture, Best Director, and Best Actor in a Leading Role.

One of the most famous scenes in the movie is when a young Forrest is being bullied by some peers, and his best friend, Jenny, encourages him to flee the situation. "Run, Forrest! Run!" became one of the film's memorable lines and is now also a popular GIF and meme.

Resilience will only be developed by rejecting Jenny's advice. Of course, if bullies are throwing rocks at you, like in the film, feel free to flee that situation. However, most of us aren't dodging rocks at the moment.

When it comes to your career, running doesn't help. In your career, running won't make you strong; it will make you weak.

You can't progress in your career without experiencing failure, hardship, setbacks, and difficulties. You can't bypass hardship. There is no loophole. It must happen; otherwise, you won't be the person you need to be when you obtain even more responsibilities.

Learning to face these difficulties head-on, rather than running, will help you develop resilience.

You might be thinking, *Well, that sounds terrible. Tell me again, why do I need resilience as an emerging leader?*

There are at least two reasons: people are not always kind, and you are not always right.

PEOPLE ARE NOT ALWAYS KIND

Leadership always involves people. Otherwise, it wouldn't be called leadership. As the great John Maxwell said so well, "He who thinks he leads, but has no followers, is only taking a walk."

People are what make leadership so rewarding and so difficult. We don't know if you've noticed this or not, but people don't have a great track record of treating each other with kindness.

I specifically remember a phone call I experienced about five years into my accounting career. I was working for a large luxury retailer, and I had to call two buyers (the professionals responsible for purchasing the merchandise to be sold in stores). My goal was to explain to them an accounting issue that would have a small, but somewhat negative, impact on their department.

I expected the call to last about five minutes, and I expected these two buyers to appreciate my time and effort. One of my expectations was correct.

The call lasted about five minutes.

It took me one minute to explain the accounting issue and the next four minutes for these two buyers to ridicule and mock me. When I got my accounting degree, I knew I wasn't going to be a "cool professional." However, I never assumed I would be insulted to my face for being an accountant. It was demoralizing, embarrassing, and confusing.

I thought we were on the same team and shared the same goal. Instead, they treated me like I was from a rival high school.

In the end, however, I did my job. I had to call them and explain this issue. That was part of my role on the team.

As I've said multiple times already, leadership is vulnerable. Sometimes you get carried off the field by your team (metaphorically speaking, of course). Sometimes you are underappreciated, get made fun of, and become the butt of jokes and the subject of gossip.

It's kind of like what Harvey Dent said in *The Dark Knight*: "You either die a hero, or you live long enough to see yourself become the villain."

I'm not predicting anyone's death. I'm just saying followers are fickle and their fickleness can lead to some hard times for you.

If you want to be a team leader, you must be able to take these punches. You must develop resilience. There is not one effective leader out there who has avoided the wrath of others. Not one.

YOU ARE NOT ALWAYS RIGHT

One of the most disheartening realities of life is that you never know what tomorrow is going to bring, as discussed in Chapter 9 (Flexibility).

Can you imagine how cool it would be to know what tomorrow is going to throw our way? You'd never be caught without an umbrella or raincoat, you'd never lose money in the stock market, and you'd have a great side-hustle gambling on sports.

Alas, you don't know what's going to happen tomorrow. This makes life both challenging and exciting. But this also makes leadership extremely difficult.

Your ignorance about tomorrow means you will never have all the information you need to make perfect decisions. Sometimes you'll make the right decision, but often you will make the wrong one.

In your professional life, wrong decisions are the equivalent of failing a test or not turning in an assignment. As an isolated event, it's probably not that big of a deal. However, if you consistently record poor scores or fail to turn in assignments, the result could be disastrous.

As a leader, you will make bad decisions. It's going to happen. Again, no leader escapes this.

I remember a time when I was leading the college ministry for my church. In the college ministry world, there are three key events every year to help you build and maintain momentum. One is a back-to-school kick-off event. Two is a fall retreat. Three is spring break.

The leader prior to me (who David worked for, by the way) was excellent at planning and executing these three events. He always chose the right events, would have a wonderful turnout, and enjoyed the momentum all year.

When I took over leading the ministry, for some reason I decided to go in a completely different direction. Rather than execute the playbook handed to me by a successful leader, I decided to blaze my own trail. I thought I knew what the students wanted, so I decided to plan all new events.

The results were embarrassing. We had about fifty people show up to our back-to-school event (compared to over five hundred the previous year). We had about nineteen students attend our fall retreat (compared to over ninety the previous year), and we had to cancel our spring break plans because only one person signed up.

Fail, fail, fail.

The interesting part of all of this was how certain I was before every event that our plan was going to be just as, if not more, successful than the previous year. I thought I knew what the students wanted and what would happen tomorrow.

I didn't.

After these failures, I had a choice: bounce back or run away. I chose to bounce back.

The team and I were able to recover from that disappointing first year. We learned a lot, adjusted our strategy, and picked up the previous leader's playbook for year two. Things with the ministry eventually got back on track, but what we learned about failure and resilience was invaluable.

If you want to progress in your career, you must learn how to bounce back from poor decisions. You will not always be right. You will make bad choices as a leader. Sometimes the consequences will be minimal; sometimes they'll be disastrous. You can't be perfect, but you can try to handle your failures perfectly by not running away.

LEADERSHIP DEMANDS RESILIENCE

You learn how to bounce back in the middle of difficult circumstances not by reading about someone else's challenges and failures, but by leaning into hardship when it comes your way.

Here are three ideas to help you become more resilient by developing a healthy appreciation for hardship.

IDEA #1: PURPOSELY LEAVE THE COMFORT ZONE

You can't always manufacture hardship, but you can choose to leave your comfort zone. This phrase became popular in the early 1990s after Judith Bardwick wrote her book *Danger in the Comfort Zone.*

"The comfort zone is a behavioral state within which a person operates in an anxiety-neutral condition, using a limited set of behaviors to deliver a steady level of performance, usually without a sense of risk."

Many people falsely believe there are only two zones in life:

1. *Comfort Zone,* where everything feels safe and controlled. Think: you on a Friday night with ice cream in your bowl, wine in your glass, and Netflix on your television.

2. *Panic Zone,* where everyone is losing their ever-loving minds. Think: the tributes at the start of the 74th Hunger Games, or if that's not your fandom, the way you reacted this morning when you woke up ten minutes before your meeting was scheduled to start.

Leaving the Comfort Zone doesn't automatically put you in the Panic Zone. Psychologists have identified four zones.[43]

1. *Comfort Zone.* As I mentioned above, you feel safe and in control.

---

43   Terri Maxwell, "Moving from the Fear Zone to the Growth Zone," Succeed on Purpose, April 20, 2020, https://www.succeedonpurpose.com/post/moving-from-the-fear-zone-to-the-growth-zone.

2. *Fear Zone.* You lack self-confidence and worry that you might not be able to succeed in a new endeavor.

3. *Learning Zone.* You face challenges head-on and develop new skills.

4. *Growth Zone.* You find purpose, set new goals, and realize your aspirations.

Let's say you recently started running for exercise and have decided to complete a marathon. This is how one might experience the four zones.

1. *Comfort Zone.* Your easy, two-mile route that you can run in less than twenty minutes and feel great.

2. *Fear Zone.* After you sign up for the marathon, you begin to wonder, *Did I just make a huge mistake?* Your simple two-mile run suddenly feels much harder. You begin to worry you don't have time to train for a full marathon, and you wonder if you will ever become one of those people with the 26.2 sticker on their vehicle.

3. *Learning Zone.* You dive in and start training. You learn how to pace yourself. How to rest after long runs. How to eat for fuel. How to take in calories during your long runs.

4. *Growth Zone.* Once you've completed the race, posted a picture of your medal on social media, and eaten an entire pizza, you reflect on what you learned, set some new goals, sign up for another race in six months, and apply your 26.2 sticker.

These four zones impact your personal life and your professional life. Whether it be taking on more responsibility, accepting a promotion before you feel ready, volunteering for a new project, or engaging in a difficult conversation with your boss, you will have ample opportunities to leave the Comfort Zone at work.

The interesting thing about moving through these zones is that no one will force you to do anything. Like what we discussed in Chapter 7, leaving the Comfort Zone requires self-leadership.

Every once in a while, someone comes along and pushes you outside of the Comfort Zone. Those people are rare, but they are also great friends.

The reality, however, remains. There is no growth in the Comfort Zone. Today's Growth Zone will be tomorrow's Comfort Zone. Those who stand out and show they are *all in* are constantly looking for ways to move through these Zones. They show they are uncomfortable with the Comfort Zone.

We are both products of the 1990s, which means we are huge fans of Jerry Seinfeld. One of the qualities we admire most about Seinfeld is how he never stops leaving the Comfort Zone. He continues to challenge himself.

After his hit television show ended, Jerry Seinfeld had more money and notoriety than he could have ever imagined. He would have had every right to sail off into the sunset feeling great about his career. He had just finished creating the most successful sitcom in the history of television. Not a bad trophy to hang on your mantel.

So what did Jerry do once his show wrapped up? He went back on the road doing stand-up.[44] Why? He didn't want to stop growing. Jerry stands out because he's always looking to leave the Comfort Zone.

So the question you need to answer is: *What is one thing I can do to step outside of my Comfort Zone?* It might be volunteering to take on a new project. Or speaking up more during team meetings. It might be engaging your team leader in a conversation about your career. Maybe hiring an executive coach. Or having a hard conversation with a coworker. It might be starting a new career or looking for a new job.

The bottom line is this: if you never leave the Comfort Zone, resilience will not be your strong suit.

IDEA #2: MAKE FRIENDS WITH THOSE WHO FAIL WHILE DARING GREATLY

In the late 1990s, Frito-Lay introduced a new line of potato chips. The brand was called WOW! The reason for this name was because these new chips were 100 percent fat-free (fat was to the '90s what gluten and carbs are to today).

Frito-Lay was excited about this new product, spending millions on marketing. However, shortly after the product launched, excitement turned to anxiety.

After the product hit the shelves, complaints started rolling in.

---

44 This was chronicled in the 2002 film *Comedian* (directed by Christian Charles, starring Jerry Seinfeld and Chris Rock, 2002)...check it out one night while sitting in your Comfort Zone.

These WOW! chips were causing some "gastrointestinal distress," if you know what we mean.

As Frito-Lay did a little exploring, they realized consumers were acting in a way they didn't expect. Consumers enjoyed these 100 percent fat-free chips so much, they were eating them by the bag-full.

Not the single-size bag you get at Subway and Jimmy John's.

The full-sized bags you get at the grocery store.

To many consumers, "low fat" meant "no limits."

The reason this was an issue is that the ingredient used to make these chips fat-free was something called olestra. "Olestra's molecules were too large to be digested by the body, passing directly through the digestive tract unabsorbed."[45] When people consumed one or two servings of olestra, most experienced no issues. But if they consumed an entire bag's worth of servings, the chips got their revenge.

The FDA stepped in and made Frito-Lay label each bag with a warning that this product might have unfortunate side effects. Not surprisingly, the general public quickly lost trust in the WOW! line of products. And the WOW! party was over shortly after it started.

---

45   Sandie Glass, "What Were They Thinking? The Chips That Sent Us Running to the Loo," *Fast Company*, January 17, 2012, https://www.fastcompany.com/1809002/what-were-they-thinking-chips-sent-us-running-loo.

Why do we share this story? So you can answer a trivia question next Tuesday night?

No, we share this story because it was a failure. Frito-Lay is a huge company full of very smart people. They left the Comfort Zone, took a risk to try something new, and it didn't go well.

Embarrassing? For sure.

Expensive? 100 percent.

Fatal to the company? Not even close.

The list of smart companies with colossal failures is extensive. Here's a list of some products you may never have heard of:

- Apple's Newton
- Nintendo's Virtual Boy
- McDonald's Arch Deluxe
- *Cosmopolitan*'s Yogurt (yes, *Cosmopolitan* the magazine)
- Microsoft's Zune
- Google's Lively
- Facebook's Home[46]

All the companies mentioned above are still in business and doing well. Failure didn't sink them—it made them stronger. That's the way life works and one of the points we're trying to make in this chapter.

---

46 Ben Gilbert, "25 of the Biggest Failed Products from the World's Biggest Companies," *Insider*, last modified October 17, 2019, https://www.businessinsider.com/biggest-product-flops-in-history-2016-12#2013-facebook-home-23.

We're not suggesting you go out with the intention to fail. That would be reckless and unwise. But it's a good idea to befriend people who have failed while also daring greatly. Why? Because perfectionists are a pain in the rear and super arrogant.

Just kidding. Here's an example of what we mean by people who have "failed while also daring greatly." In April of 1910, former president Theodore Roosevelt gave one of the most famous speeches of his career. The official title of the speech was "Citizenship of a Republic," but it is now commonly referred to as "The Man in the Arena." In this speech, Roosevelt says this:

> It is not the critic who counts; not the man who points out how the strong man stumbles, or where the doer of deeds could have done them better. The credit belongs to the man who is actually in the arena...who at the worst, if he fails, at least fails while daring greatly, so that his place shall never be with those cold and timid souls who neither know victory nor defeat.[47]

If you purposely leave the Comfort Zone, there will be times when things do not go well. There will be times when you fail. It's not a matter of if, but when. To not suffer defeat by these inevitable mishaps and failures, I suggest you make friends with others who have left the Comfort Zone and, despite also experiencing failure, did so while daring greatly.

Making friends with those who have failed will help you deal with your own failures more effectively. If you spend time with people who have failed, two things happen:

---

47   Erin McCarthy, "Roosevelt's 'The Man in the Arena,'" *Mental Floss*, April 25, 2015, https://www. mentalfloss.com/article/63389/roosevelts-man-arena.

- It reminds you how often failure happens.
- It reminds you how often people bounce back.

Sheryl Sandberg has been one of the most successful and well-known women in business over the last twenty years. A handful of her accomplishments include these:

- Chief operating officer at Meta
- Founder of LeanIn.org
- First woman to be elected to serve on the board of directors for Meta
- Chief of staff for U.S. Treasury Secretary Lawrence Summers
- Harvard graduate
- Net worth of approximately $1.8 billion (yes, billion, with a "b")

If you read her list of accomplishments and accolades, you might think Sheryl was born with a silver spoon in her mouth and life has always been easy. Well, you'd be wrong.

In April 2017, Sheryl Sandberg and Adam Grant published a book called *Option B: Facing Adversity, Building Resilience, and Finding Joy.* This book chronicles an unexpected aspect of Sheryl's story.

In May of 2015, while on a vacation, her husband died suddenly, leaving her and their two children heartbroken and confused. In her story, she doesn't just talk about recovering from unexpected tragedy. She also talks about all the bumps she experienced on her road to healing. Bumps like calling people by their wrong name, talking in circles at meetings, making some iffy work decisions.

As you read her book, you realize how often failure happens and how often people bounce back. These stories are helpful and give us all hope.

Sheryl isn't alone either. Kevin Hart, Phil Knight, Matthew McConaughey, Steve Martin, Martin Short, and Tina Fey all have stories of failure that led to resilience, and resilience leading them to success.

To be clear, you don't have to read books to remind yourself of how failure builds resilience. Every single person on the face of this planet has failed. It's common to the human experience.

However, what's not common is the way people respond to failure. Some shut down, quit, and develop debilitating insecurities. Others take notes, learn lessons, and keep moving forward.

Next time you get together with friends, ask them, "What is one failure you've experienced, and how has that failure made you more resilient?"

If someone in your friend group doesn't have an answer, I suggest quickly voting them off your friend island. As you look to develop your EDGE and stand out, you don't need to hang out with perfect people.

You need to hang out with people who are not afraid to leave the Comfort Zone. People who are not going to cower in the face of adversity, but instead take risks and become resilient.

IDEA #3: WATCH OUT FOR FEAR AND SHAME

Back in the day, I used to call myself a runner. That was my preferred form of physical activity. I ran three to four days a week and completed over ten half-marathons and two full marathons.

One of the lessons I learned early in my running phase was the first mile always sucks. Always. I always felt like quitting during the first mile. I never experienced a "runner's high" during mile one. That always came later.

I know my experience was not isolated. Any runner I've ever talked to has the same experience. I wasn't proud to complete a three-mile, five-mile, or ten-mile run. I was proud that I didn't quit during mile one. *That* was the real accomplishment.

When things felt uncomfortable, that's when I was tempted to run away from my run. However, because I didn't quit during mile one, my body was able to develop endurance and resilience. The same is true for us professionally.

As we mentioned at the beginning of the chapter, one of the main reasons more aspiring professionals do not develop resilience is because when things at the office or on their team get difficult, they say "peace out" and run, rather than stay patient.

The largest barrier between you and resilience is you. Life is going to throw failure and hardship your way. That's inevitable. You will experience difficult times in your career. You are going to make bad decisions, have a terrible boss, work with annoying peers, face stiff competition, make a client angry, and experience market fluctuations.

The opportunities to develop resilience are plentiful. However, just because the opportunities are plentiful doesn't mean developing resilience is inevitable. The temptation to run will be strong.

There are two times when the temptation to run will be the strongest. When you feel fear and when you feel shame.

In the same way that a new year causes thousands of people to start running to lose weight and stay in shape, fear and shame cause thousands of professionals to run and lose the opportunity to develop resilience.

According to Webster's, fear is the unpleasant emotion caused by being aware of danger, and shame is the painful emotion caused by the consciousness of guilt, shortcoming, or impropriety.

Let me share a quick story. Back in 2006, I had just started a new job with an accounting firm in the Dallas area. I was performing an audit for a new client. The main accountant for this new client wasn't too impressive. Let's call him Scott (though that is not his name).

Scott was a kind and hard-working man, but he didn't have an accounting degree and didn't really know what he was doing. Scott had started with this company when things were simple. As the company grew, so did the complexity of their accounting. He was struggling to keep up, which made the audit challenging.

We were nearing the finish line of the audit. We were putting together the financial statements and needed someone to write a complex footnote explaining a complicated aspect of their accounting procedures.

Technically, as the auditor, I couldn't write the footnote for the client. This meant someone from the client needed to draft this footnote. I communicated this to Scott via email.

A few hours later, I received an email from Scott with a beautifully written footnote. I mean it was amazing. I was shocked.

So what did I do? I forwarded it to my bosses and said (with a snarky tone), "Wow, this is a sophisticated footnote. I wonder if Scott wrote this or if the CEO did?"

About ten minutes later, another email from Scott hit my inbox. He said, "Well, yes, I did ask the CEO to help me write it."

My heart sank. Scott wasn't supposed to read my snarky comment.

I scrolled down and realized I had made a terrible mistake. I thought I hit "forward" on the email containing the most beautifully written footnote ever. Instead, I hit "reply."

My snarky comment didn't go to my bosses. My snarky comment went directly to the client!

In that moment, I was feeling fear and shame. Fear because I realized I had just offended a client and, therefore, could be fired in an instant. Shame because I was conscious of my guilt, shortcoming, and impropriety.

At that moment, I wanted to run. Fear and shame are two strong emotions.

I was experiencing pain similar to a "first-mile pain." This meant I had a decision to make: do I lean into this and own up to my mistake or do I cover it up, try to blame someone, or make up an excuse for my behavior?

What would you do?

Well, I chose to lean into this situation and own up to my shortcoming.

I called my boss and told him what had happened. What was his reaction? Laughter. That felt good, but also added to my shame.

He basically said, "Adam, that was not a smart move, but what Scott doesn't know is your tone. One of the great things about email is it's just words. The reader can't detect tone or body language. I would just send him a note back encouraging him and thanking him for sending us the footnote. Let's try to wrap this audit up. And, Adam, don't ever do this again. Think before you hit send."

Great advice.

If you want to develop resilience, then you need to learn to read your own emotional warning signs. Fear and shame are like the lights on the dashboard of your car. They let you know something is going on and needs to be addressed.

As a leader, failure and mistakes are inevitable—maturity is not making fewer mistakes, it's facing your mistakes head-on.

One way to build resilience is by resisting the urge to run when you feel fear or shame. Fear and shame are normal emotions you will experience during your leadership journey. Feeling these emotions does not necessarily indicate that you need to leave your job. When you face whatever is causing these emotions, you develop character.

Anyone who has climbed the ladder has made mistakes. They've all sent dumb emails, said stupid things, made poor judgment calls, missed deadlines, etc. They aren't successful because they're perfect. They're successful because they're resilient and resisted the urge to run.

FAILURE IS INEVITABLE, RESILIENCE IS OPTIONAL

If there was a definitive ranking of best leaders in American history, without a doubt, Abraham Lincoln's name would appear on that list. Healing the nation after the Civil War and emancipating those who were horrendously enslaved is a stellar track record. He deserves to be on any "greatest leaders" list.

However, if you Google "Lincoln's failures" you'll also see quite the list. Lost elections, deaths of loved ones, and struggles with anxiety. It's a sobering list.

Lincoln's journey is more typical than we're comfortable admitting. As we just said above, great leaders who find their EDGE and stand out are resilient. They have been treated poorly by others, they have made terrible decisions, but they didn't run. They didn't give up. They didn't stop because things got hard.

The reward for stick-to-itiveness is character. This means even if your resilience doesn't cause you to stand out by showing you're *all in*, even if your resilience doesn't give your career an EDGE, it's still worth it.

It's worth it because you will become a person of character. Someone who is not easily deterred. Someone who doesn't run. Someone who is willing to look hardship in the face.

If that happens, you win. No matter what or where your career goes, you win.

CHAPTER 11

PEACEMAKER

USEFUL INFORMATION...YESTERDAY

The 1998 film *The Wedding Singer* tells the story of two people (Robbie, played by Adam Sandler, and Julia, played by Drew Barrymore) who were engaged to be married to the wrong people. Fortune intervenes and helps them discover one another. We totally ripped that off from IMDb. That's not the way we talk.

It's a classic rom-com with predictable plot twists and a happy ending. Sometimes, those kinds of movies are just what the doctor ordered.

Robbie's broken engagement is significantly more dramatic than Julia's. The film opens at Robbie's wedding ceremony where he is awkwardly stood up at the altar in front of all his friends and family. It's a tense scene that's made slightly less tense by Adam Sandler's silly faces and a healthy dose of '80s music.

When Robbie finally gets to discuss this situation with his

ex-fiancée, Linda, he lets her know he's still willing to marry her if she needs just "a little more time."

Linda's response: "No, I don't need more time, Robbie. I don't ever want to marry you."

Robbie looks hurt, but calmly responds, "Jeez, you know, that information might have been a little more useful to me yesterday."

Linda then goes on to drop truth bomb after truth bomb on poor Robbie. She lets him know she liked him better six years ago, she doesn't like his current job, she doesn't like the way he dresses, and that ultimately, she's afraid marrying him will keep her forever trapped in their small town.

Robbie's finally had enough and yells, "Once again, things that could have been brought to my attention *yesterday*!"

DON'T BE LINDA

This is going to sound a little crazy, but there's a lesson to learn in the opening scene of this rom-com classic. The lesson is this: resolve your conflicts sooner rather than later. Holding back what *needs* to be said usually backfires. As Kim Scott says, "Unspoken feedback always explodes like a dirty bomb."

Although it was great for Linda to finally discuss what she felt about her relationship, the timing was horrible.

You can certainly empathize with Linda. Awkward conversations are rarely fun, but you shouldn't handle them how she did.

If you are going to stand out by showing you're *all in*, then you will need to develop some peacemaking skills. You'll need to learn how to lean into awkward and difficult conversations. No leader will achieve any level of success without first learning how to navigate difficult conflicts.

THE BAD NEWS ABOUT CONFLICT

Conflict is inevitable *and* necessary.

Inevitable because you work with humans, and humans have a terrible track record when it comes to getting along. *Necessary* because sometimes you need a robust debate and diversity of thought to make a project or final product excellent.

Simply put, you won't make it far if you keep running from conflict. You also won't be healthy if you keep stifling what needs to be said.

When I share this idea with leaders, I am often met with one of two reactions.

- There is always one group of people saying, "Hell yeah, conflict is necessary!" This may come as a surprise to some of you, but some people are not bothered at all by conflict. In fact, if they have a hard or difficult conversation, it makes their day. Those people typically host political talk shows and have no friends, but they do exist. Of course, I'm kidding. I'm not on that side of the conflict preference spectrum, so that was my passive-aggressive way of making fun of those people.
- There is another group of people who, when faced with conflict, say, "I'd rather pull out my nose hairs, one by one."

Again, I feel the pain of this group because this is me. I'll talk about this more later, but I am one of the biggest conflict avoiders I know. Because I am a natural conflict avoider, and I understand full well the pain many conflict avoiders feel, I have the moral authority to say what I'm about to say. Conflict avoiding is wrong.

Conflict is not the end of your world. In fact, I'll go one step further: engaging in healthy and productive conflict is one way to make your world (and the world at large) better.

This doesn't mean you need to pick fights on social media. It simply means if you make some slight adjustments to your perspective and learn some peacemaking tools, conflict won't ruin your day. It might even make it better.

NOT ALL CONFLICT IS THE SAME

There are two types of conflicts in the world, and knowing the difference between the two helps. There is "task-related conflict" and "personal conflict."

Task-related conflict means working through differing ideas and perspectives on work-related items. Amy Gallo, a contributing editor at the *Harvard Business Review*, is a fan of task-related conflict.

"You might dream of working in a peaceful utopia, but it wouldn't be good for your company, your work, or you. In fact, disagreements—when managed well—have lots of positive outcomes."[48]

---

48 Amy Gallo, "Why We Should Be Disagreeing More at Work," *Harvard Business Review*, January 3, 2018, https://hbr.org/2018/01/why-we-should-be-disagreeing-more-at-work#:~:text=Improved%20relationships.,fights%20and%20then%20move%20on.

She goes on to list better outcomes, like more creative solutions to problems, opportunities to learn and grow, improved relationships, higher job satisfaction, and a more inclusive work environment.

Unfortunately, sometimes task-related conflicts can become personal conflicts, which is when arguing over a work-related item begins to negatively impact your relationship with another person or when your feelings get hurt during a task-related conflict. Personal conflict can be exhausting, but it, too, can lead to positive outcomes (getting to know people better, learning more about yourself, and developing humility).

Most professionals never receive any formal training on how to handle task-related or personal conflict. We want to change that. This is an exhaustive topic worth additional reading and research, but the remainder of this chapter will serve as a great primer.

First, we will encourage you to learn your go-to conflict ditch. Second, we'll share a great question to ask when conflict arises. Last, we'll discuss why we believe most of the authority figures you met in your youth might have led you astray when it comes to properly ending a conflict.

IDEA #1: LEARN YOUR CONFLICT DITCH

When it comes to conflict, many people have a few bad habits. It's these bad habits that make difficult conversations so difficult. According to researchers at the University of Denver, the four most common bad habits are as follows: withdrawal, escalation, negative interpretation, and invalidation.[49]

---

49   Scott Stanley et al., *A Lasting Promise: The Christian Guide to Fighting for Your Marriage* (Hoboken, NJ: Jossey-Bass, 1998).

1. *Withdrawal* is the unwillingness to stay in a difficult conversation. Withdrawal could be expressed by literally walking out of the room or hanging up on someone. However, most of the time it's expressed by ignoring tension, shutting down emotionally during a hard conversation, holding back what you really want to say, or saying only 90 percent of what needs to be said.

   In professional environments, withdrawal is most often experienced as withholding feedback. For example, when a professional is frustrated by the actions of a colleague but doesn't share their frustration because they want to "keep the peace" or "it will be awkward."

2. *Escalation* is what causes interpersonal conflict to get ugly. This happens when one person tries to win, at all costs. Harsh things are said. Insults are made. Emotions run hot, and voices get loud.

   In professional environments, escalation is most often experienced as yelling and arguing. It most often happens in meetings when teams are trying to make a decision that involves multiple opinions. In these situations, people can sometimes develop "idea bias" (i.e., they fall in love with their own idea) and fight hard to make sure their idea is the winning idea. When coworkers escalate, the tension is palpable. It can be awkward and uncomfortable for those in the room.

3. *Negative interpretation* happens when you believe you know the motives and thoughts of other people. Your beliefs about people's motives then become the lens by which you interpret all their actions.

In professional environments, negative interpretation is most often experienced as the slow erosion of trust. When you believe the motives and intentions of a person are negative, it's difficult to build a healthy relationship with that person. Negative interpretation leads to imposter syndrome, feeling insecure about your role on a team, and the belief that people are "trying to keep you down."

4. *Invalidation* happens when one person belittles another. When your thoughts, feelings, or ideas are discounted or insulted, that's invalidation. If you've ever been told you "shouldn't feel that way" or "that's dumb," that's invalidation.

   In professional environments, invalidation is most often experienced when someone tells another person they shouldn't be feeling whatever emotion they are feeling. If someone says they are feeling something negative while at work, many professionals treat those situations the same way you would treat a cockroach making an appearance at a dinner party you're hosting at your apartment. Isolate and destroy!

So why do I share these four negative communication patterns? It's important to be able to identify and address when one of these is negatively impacting you and your team. Those who climb the corporate ladder know how to navigate the relational complexities of organizational life.

Let me share some of my own personal research. I've been teaching the WENI principle (withdrawal, escalation, negative interpretation, and invalidation) to professionals for over a decade. I love the looks on their faces when I teach these four common patterns. It's a mixture of amazement and frustration.

They react like Robbie. "Once again, things that could have been brought to my attention *yesterday*!" They are amazed at how helpful Dr. Stanley's work is to their life and frustrated that no one taught them the WENI principle sooner. "Once again, things that could have been brought to my attention in *high school*!"

After I teach the principles, I ask the audience to force rank the four patterns from bad to worst. All the patterns can be unhelpful to relationships, but I'm always curious to know which one they believe is the worst of the worst.

According to the professionals I've worked with, here is how most of them force rank WENI from worst of the worst to least of the worst:

1. Escalation

2. Invalidation

3. Negative interpretation

4. Withdrawal

Most professionals believe escalation is the "worst of the worst." This makes a lot of sense. "Professionalism" is highly valued in organizational life. "Professionalism" is often a subtle way to say, "Don't ever lose control of your emotions." So whenever a professional thinks about someone "losing control of their emotions," that's generally taboo.

Dr. Stanley's team has also done a force ranking. His research ranks the worst of the worst as withdrawal, not escalation. The exact opposite of what most professionals believe.

Why is withdrawal the worst of the worst? Because when someone withdraws, there is no communication. When communication has shut down, things can't get better. Withdrawal has ruined more relationships, professional and personal, than any of the other four negative communication patterns.

What's even crazier, Dr. Stanley's research identifies escalation as the best of the worst. Why? Because when people are escalating, at least they are still talking.

No problem will ever be resolved by ignoring it. If two people are in conflict, they must stay in the ring and keep talking. To be clear, escalation is still a negative communication pattern. It can cause damage and make things difficult, but it's better than not talking.

If your ditch is withdrawal, you need to learn how to gather your thoughts and stick with a conversation.

If your ditch is escalation, you need to learn how to breathe deeply and keep the conversation from emotionally getting out of hand.

If your ditch is negative interpretation, you need to learn how to get curious and not assign intent to people.

If your ditch is invalidation, you need to learn how to empathize with others and understand their feelings aren't something you can control.

I'll say it again: conflict isn't bad. It's inevitable, and it's necessary. As an emerging leader, you must learn how to face it without it ruining your day.

Brené Brown's writing has been helpful, especially as it relates to this topic. Her team uses the term "rumble" as a way to describe these hard conversations:

> A rumble is a discussion, conversation, or meeting defined by a commitment to lean into vulnerability, to stay curious and generous, to stick with the messy middle of problem identification and solving, to take a break and circle back when necessary, to be fearless in owning our parts, and, as psychologist Harriet Lerner teaches, to listen with the same passion with which we want to be heard.[50]

Whether you call it social awareness, rumbling, or peacemaking, successful leaders work hard to navigate awkward conversations. These conversations are never easy, but they are important. Leadership involves people, and people butt heads, make mistakes, act selfishly, and need feedback and coaching.

As a leader, you simply cannot avoid difficult conversations. You will either develop the necessary abilities to navigate these conversations with wisdom or you will not be someone who leads. Those are your two options.

IDEA #2: FOCUS ON THEIR VERSION OF THE FACTS

You know what often makes conflict so frustrating? Two people rarely agree on what happened. If you were to jump into the con-

---

50 Brené Brown, "Let's Rumble," *Brené Brown* (blog), May 1, 2019, https://brenebrown.com/blog/2019/05/01/lets-rumble/.

versation between Robbie and Linda from *The Wedding Singer* to help them reconcile, one of the first questions you might ask is, "So, Robbie, Linda, thank you for allowing me to help you two try to reconcile. I'll start with this question: what happened?"

It's a simple question but, oddly enough, very difficult to agree on. In fact, many people in conflict *stay* in conflict because they can never agree on the answer to this question.

This is how the authors of *Difficult Conversations* describe this simple question:

"The 'What Happened?' Conversation is where we spend much of our time in difficult conversations as we struggle with our different stories about who's right, who meant what, and who's to blame."[51]

They are right.

Conflict is complicated. There are layers. There is nuance. There is detail. All of this means the facts of the conflict can often be fuzzy.

If you are in a conflict with someone, if someone frustrated or hurt you, or you frustrated or hurt someone else, rather than beginning the conflict by arguing your version of the facts, it's better to start off by asking, "From your perspective, what happened?"

Asking someone to share their version of the facts doesn't mean

---

51 Douglas Stone, Bruce Patton, and Sheila Heen, *Difficult Conversations: How to Discuss What Matters Most* (London: Penguin Books, 2011), reprint, 9.

you agree with them; it simply means you are trying to understand the situation from their perspective.

This is exactly why so many conflicts rage for so long: both parties are fighting hard to be understood. People almost never change their perspectives without first feeling understood.[52] So resolving a conflict doesn't start with demanding the other party understand you, it starts with you seeking to understand the other party.

Again, seeking to understand doesn't mean you are being soft or agreeing to their version of the facts, it simply means you are seeking to understand. Something really strange and unexpected happens when you seek to understand. You realize that most people are reasonable. Meaning: they do things for a reason.

When you understand how someone viewed the source of the conflict, then typically, the emotions they felt make more sense.

"Oh, you thought I was mad that you missed the deadline, and that's why your response was so defensive."

"Okay, that makes sense. You read my email as me expressing my disappointment with you, so that's why you were so reserved and shut-off during our meeting."

"I get it. When I consistently showed up late to our scheduled meetings, you assumed I was big-timing you and didn't care about your time. That's why you've been so frustrated with me the past few weeks."

---

52 Stone, Patton, and Heen, *Difficult Conversations*, 29.

So if you want to become a conflict resolution ninja, put away the sharp sword and start by asking a different question: "From your perspective, what happened?"

IDEA #3: LEARN HOW TO APOLOGIZE, LIKE AN ADULT

Chances are high that while you were growing up, you were taught an incorrect way to resolve a conflict. Let us explain.

Think back to your middle school years, and imagine it was a rainy day during the summer, so you and your brother were playing *Mario Kart*. You've been dominating your brother all morning with Toad. He's been trailing behind you because he, once again, decided to race with Donkey Kong. You challenge your brother to a winner-take-all race, and he accepts.

The light turns green, and you immediately jump out front and stay there for two and a half laps.

Then, a series of unfortunate events take place: the blue shell seeks you out and flips you upside down, Wario comes up behind you and hits you with another turtle shell, slowing you even further, then just as the finish line is in sight, Donkey Kong (i.e., your little brother) comes flying up behind you on Bullet Bill. He passes you across the finish line and wins the race.

Your brother absolutely loses his mind! He begins dancing, yelling, and singing. Then it's the typical childhood scene: "I beat you!" "I let you win!" "No, you didn't. I won! I won! I won!"

At this point, you've had enough. You are still holding the game controller in your hand, and you instinctively throw it at your brother.

As the controller flies through the air, everyone's eyes widen.

You are shocked at how quickly the controller appears to be moving and equally shocked at how precisely the controller hits your brother in the exact middle of his forehead.

Once your brother recovers from his injury, your babysitter brings you two together to reconcile. What did the babysitter demand you say to your brother?

That's right. "I'm sorry."

It's a classic. It's simple. It's pithy. It's been used for years. Unfortunately, however, it's not the end of a conflict. In fact, saying "I'm sorry" is really one of the worst ways to end a conflict.

We know, you might be feeling that tinge of distrust toward authority figures—like what you felt when you realized there was no tooth fairy or your Uncle Steve was an alcoholic rather than naturally happy all the time.

This conflict "ended" the way most conflicts attempt to end—with an apology. Apologies are definitely part of the conflict reconciliation process, but they are not the definitive end of the process.

When you say, "I'm sorry," what you are really doing is expressing what you are feeling. It's just like saying, "I'm happy," "I'm tired," or "I'm hungry." When you say you're sorry, you're telling the other person, "I feel bad for what I did to you."

It's great to express that remorse—however, that doesn't give the person you hurt or frustrated anything to work with. They can't do anything with your feelings.

In the ridiculous example above, when your brother is sitting there with a lump on his forehead, expressing your emotions doesn't help. Your brother doesn't need to focus on you, he needs someone to focus on him.

What's true in your personal life is also true in your professional life.

When you miss a deadline, accidentally send a snarky email to a client, get snippy with a coworker, or miss a typo in an important proposal, an expression of your remorse doesn't fix anything or move you closer to reconciling with the person you hurt, disappointed, or frustrated.

So what should you do if you don't say "I'm sorry"? We like what Ken Sande, a trained lawyer and mediator, suggests. In his book *The Peacemaker*, he provides a list of "Seven As" to guide you as you seek to reconcile with someone you've hurt or frustrated.

1. Ask others for help with self-awareness.

2. Address everyone involved in the conflict.

3. Avoid "if, but, or maybe." Don't excuse your behavior. Be specific.

4. Apologize.

5. Ask for forgiveness.

6. Accept the consequences.

7. Alter your behavior.

Let's say you put together a slide deck to be used during an important business development meeting, and it contained numerous errors. Here is how you could work through the steps listed above.

Ask others on your team, "Do I do this often? Do you see me miss details?"

Address the coworkers who were in the meeting and negatively impacted by your errors. Let your coworkers know the errors were your mistake.

Avoid, "if, but, or maybe." Own the mistake.

Apologize and let the coworkers know how you feel.

Ask the coworkers to forgive you for the error.

Accept whatever consequences that might be offered.

Alter your behavior. Maybe you double- and triple-check future slide decks. Maybe you don't volunteer for those detail-oriented projects any longer. Maybe it just involves slowing down. Whatever it is, let others know how you plan to alter your behavior to avoid this in the future.

I know, that seems like a lot. You might also be thinking, *Who on earth does that?* My answer is not many. This is a book about how to stand out, and to stand out you have to do what most people won't.

Think about someone who has hurt or frustrated you. Isn't this what you want them to do? Don't you want them to own their mistake, not make excuses, recognize how their behavior negatively impacted you, accept consequences, and alter their behavior?

Wouldn't you be impressed if someone had the character and confidence to own their mistakes like that? Wouldn't that cause you to trust that person *more*, not *less*? Would that person stand out? Of course, they would.

So if your task conflict becomes personal conflict, walk through the seven As.

One side note. We know you might be wondering, *Great advice, but what if the person I'm in conflict with is the one who has done all the hurting? What if I'm a victim of someone else's poor behavior, and they are the one who needs to walk through the seven As?*

We get this question often. One downside of learning a healthier way of dealing with relational conflict is that you start to realize how few people know how to deal with it in a healthy way.

Dealing with unreasonable people or people who don't care about reconciling conflict can be very challenging and is beyond the scope of this book.

Two quick thoughts:

1. You can only faithfully let people know when they've hurt or frustrated you, but you can't force anyone to work the seven steps.

2. Every bit of relational conflict is unique and nuanced. A few principles are universal, but in the end, it's impossible to define next steps without learning the details.

It's useful in those situations to find someone to help process the conflict. Not to gossip about the person, but to genuinely seek advice and counsel from others. You could say to a trusted friend or coworker, "I'm in conflict with a person at work, and I don't know the best way to address it. Will you allow me to explain the situation so you can help me come up with a plan?"

If you would like to do some additional research, we point you to Ken Sande's book (*The Peacemaker*) as well as the book quoted above, *Difficult Conversations*. These resources are a great place to start and address these types of situations in more detail.

SUCKY MOVIES

Pixar has an impressive track record of hit animated films.

I was part of the Walt Disney College Program in 1995 when *Toy Story* was released in theaters. I will never forget watching that film. Pixar's computer animation technique was something never used in a feature-length film, so I expected the final product to be visually stunning, but thin on plot.

I was wrong.

Pixar didn't just make a great-*looking* film—they made a great film. I didn't expect to be emotionally engaged in the plot, but I was. That combination of amazing visuals and engaging stories has served Pixar well over the last twenty-five years.

After Pixar released *Finding Nemo* in 2003, it was clear they had figured something out. It looked like they had the Hollywood version of the Midas touch because every film they released became a box office and critical success.

As an outside observer of the company, I assumed the reason for their success was talent. I assumed they had simply gotten lucky and hired the best people. And when those "best people" got together, they made hit movies.

Once again, I was wrong.

According to Ed Catmull, one of the founders of Pixar, the reason for the animation studio's success was not just due to talent (although he quickly admits they have been lucky to hire some very talented people). The reason for their success is task-related conflict.

In Catmull's book *Creativity, Inc.*, he said something that was equal parts fascinating and relieving. He said that every Pixar film starts off as an "ugly baby."

> This is why I call early mock-ups of our films 'ugly babies.' They are not beautiful, miniature versions of the adults they will grow up to be. They are truly ugly: awkward and unformed, vulnerable

and incomplete. They need nurturing—in the form of time and patience—in order to grow.[53]

So how does a Pixar film move from ugly baby to smash hit?

Something called the Braintrust.

> We rely on the Braintrust to push us toward excellence and to root out mediocrity. The Braintrust, which meets every few months or so to assess each movie we're making, is our primary delivery system for straight talk. Its premise is simple: put smart, passionate people in a room together, charge them with identifying and solving problems, and encourage them to be candid with one another.[54]

Why did Pixar institutionalize task-related conflict? Ed Catmull would say it's because "early on, all of our movies suck."

Pixar didn't gain an edge in Hollywood because they lucked out on hiring a bunch of talented people. They gained an edge because they had the humility to recognize talent alone doesn't produce greatness.

They purposely asked for feedback from others and weren't afraid to lean into difficult conversations. They weren't afraid to speak candidly to one another.

I'm confident the Braintrust is awkward and painful the first few times you participate. Willingly opening yourself up to feedback,

---

53   Ed Catmull and Amy Wallace, *Creativity, Inc.: Overcoming the Unseen Forces That Stand in the Way of True Inspiration* (New York: Penguin Random House, 2014), Kindle edition, 131.

54   Catmull and Wallace, *Creativity, Inc.*, 86–87.

especially from people you know and trust, takes courage and vulnerability.

However, just because Pixar institutionalized task-related conflict doesn't make it easy to hear challenging feedback. The filmmakers had to develop the endurance necessary to engage in these conversations.

The box office results and critical acclaim are proof the courage and vulnerability were worth it. They were rewarded for their endurance.

I resonate with the Pixar story because, in many ways, it's my story. No, making animated films is not my side hustle. I have benefited from candid feedback and task-related conflict.

As I mentioned above, I'm a self-proclaimed conflict avoider. Left to my own wishes and preferences, I would never—and by never I mean *never*—engage in hard conversations.

The ostrich with its head in the sand is my preferred way of living. I was all about "you do you and I'll do me" long before that idea became cool.

For whatever reason, I encountered leaders and managers early in my career who cared enough to help me see how much better things would be once I pulled my head out of the sand.

It was painful at first to hear constructive feedback on my work and how I was to work with.

It felt awkward to give candid feedback on other people's work and how they were to work with.

But then something amazing happened.

Over time, I began to fear these conversations less and less. I began to understand that although these difficult conversations are not my preference, they are extremely important. I was able to develop the endurance necessary to navigate these conversations, and I can sit here today and say this is one of the areas where I've experienced the most professional and personal growth over the last twenty years.

What's true for Pixar has been true for me, and it's probably true for you too. Your talent alone will not help you achieve the results you want. You need to get comfortable with conflict. You need to develop the art of speaking with candor and become skilled at peacemaking.

Appreciate task-related conflict, and when task-related conflict turns personal, have the skills to reconcile and resolve those personal conflicts.

I can't promise it will be easy or that you'll ever get comfortable with these conversations, but I can promise that they will freak you out less and less, and you'll be able to look back on your career and see the positive results of growing in this area.

CHAPTER 12

PATIENCE

DAD, I JUST GET SO BORED

My wife and I have two boys. At the time of this writing, one is a seventh grader, and the other is a fifth grader. My wife and I seem to have the exact same conversation with our fifth grader every night. And by every night, I mean...Every. Single. Night.

The conversation goes something like this:

Us: Please, go brush your teeth. And be sure to do it for two minutes!

Son: Okay. *Leaves room.*

Forty-eight seconds later, comes running back into the room.

Son: Done!

Us: No, you are not. That was not two minutes.

Son: Yes, it was.

Us: Son, you are doing fine in school, and I know you know how to tell time. That was not two minutes. Get back in there, now.

Son: Fine. *Leaves room again.*

About ninety seconds later, comes back into the room.

Son: Okay, *now* I'm done.

Every. Night.

We've tried everything to stop having this conversation. Incentives, a watch with a countdown timer, toothbrushes with countdown timers. Nothing works.

This happened again a few weeks ago. I was tired of this conversation, so I sat him down and asked, "Why is this a struggle? You end up brushing your teeth twice every night because you won't brush for two minutes the first time. I'm sure you don't want to have this conversation any more than I do. So, can you help me understand? Why is it so hard to brush your teeth for two minutes?"

He sat there and thought for a moment, and then blurted out, "Dad, I just get so bored."

Suddenly, it all made so much sense.

I looked at him and said, "Ah. Okay, I get it. I get it."

My son is learning to navigate an important aspect of life: how to battle boredom.

Nowadays, we can all relate to this struggle with boredom. If you stop and think about it, two minutes is an eternity to do nothing but stare at your face in the mirror.

When my son said the reason he struggles to brush for two minutes is that he gets bored, I totally understood, and I felt sorry for him. I, too, hate feeling bored. It's the worst.

I haven't been bored in over eleven years. I remember the last day I was bored. It was in early April 2010, the day *before* I got my first iPhone. When I'm faced with a boring situation, I just pull out my iPhone.

- Sitting at a stoplight. No big deal, I'll check my email.
- Waiting in line at the grocery store. Who cares? I can text my friends.
- Elevator rides with strangers. Not a problem, I'll read the day's news headlines.
- Walking from the parking lot to my office building. No sweat, I'll review my calendar.
- Commercial breaks during my favorite TV shows. I'm not concerned, I can shop on Amazon.
- Brushing my teeth. I can repeat any of the items listed above.

My trusty little iPhone is always there to help me fight through the boring little mundane moments of my day.

GOLDFISH AND THE RITZ-CARLTON

Question: do you feel like your attention span is longer or shorter than it was ten years ago?

Most of the people we talk to believe their attention span is decreasing, not increasing. Some anecdotal evidence out there supports this notion.

In 2015, Microsoft conducted a study on attention spans. Their conclusion: "people now generally lose concentration after eight seconds, highlighting the effects of an increasingly digitalized lifestyle on the brain."[55] Microsoft conducted this same study in 2000, and they determined the average attention span at that time was twelve seconds. In fifteen years, that's about a 30 percent decrease.

And, in case you are wondering, eight seconds is less than the attention span of a goldfish. I'm not sure how a goldfish's attention span was measured (or why it was measured), but a child's pet will now pay attention to you longer than an adult.

In a 2017 interview with the former president and COO of the Ritz-Carlton, Horst Schulze, he told an interesting story. In 1983 when the brand opened its first hotel in the Buckhead neighborhood of Atlanta, GA., they studied how long it would take a guest to get irritated while waiting in line to check into the hotel. In 1983, that number was four minutes. If a guest was waiting longer than four minutes, a member of the staff would come and greet them while in line and offer them something to eat or drink to pass the time.

---

55   Kevin McSpadden, "You Now Have a Shorter Attention Span Than a Goldfish," *Time*, May 14, 2015, https://time.com/3858309/attention-spans-goldfish/.

In 2017, that number had shrunk to twenty seconds. Twenty seconds! That's a significant change in thirty-four years.

A NEW SKILL FOR A NEW ERA

Shortening attention spans and boredom intolerance are not unique to fifth graders. These are issues for all of us, and they are having an impact on not just our personal lives, but our professional lives as well.

One of the more practical skills needed to succeed today is the ability to keep yourself focused. The ability to manage your own attention span.

If you can learn how to focus your attention and stay engaged in your work, it's almost guaranteed you'll stand out. Focusing on hard things—things that might be a tad boring—will help you develop patience. In today's fast-paced culture, patience is rare, but many great things patiently develop over time, not overnight (e.g., wine, coffee, bourbon, trees, mountains, prosciutto, Matthew McConaughey's acting career).

Three ideas to help you learn how to focus your attention and develop patience.

IDEA #1: INTENTIONALLY TIMEBOX MOMENTS TO BUILD YOUR ATTENTION ENDURANCE (I.E., GET CRAP DONE)

When it comes to developing patience by staying focused, your calendar can be your best friend. I have met countless leaders who complain about not being able to get anything done because they are in meetings all day. What this means is their attention is constantly changing from one thing to another, and they rarely have time to focus on an idea for longer than a few minutes.

Over time, this can be detrimental. If a runner wants to build endurance, they run (crazy, huh?). In the same way, you must give yourself time to build your "attention endurance"—time during the day to focus on deep work and get done what you need to get done.

Successful leaders understand they can't be in meetings all day, every day. They must find time to think, work, and create. However, they don't blame the people who invite them to meetings or those who "stop by for a quick question." They don't wait for other people to care about their calendar. They take the initiative to block out time during their day to get stuff done, and—pay attention, because this is the key—they *honor* the time they've blocked off.

The lesson for you is this: the sooner you can start purposely scheduling time for yourself to get things done, the better. If you don't earmark time for yourself, someone else will almost always grab that time and invite you to an "important meeting."

Want to know the fastest way to burn out? Never allow yourself to get any work done during normal working hours. Say yes to every meeting and every quick conversation, and tell yourself, *I can get to my to-do list tonight* or *I'll get caught up this weekend.* Do that consistently, and sooner or later you'll find yourself sitting in your team leader's office with tears and snot running down your face saying, "I just can't do it anymore!"

One of the questions often asked when discussing the power of timeboxing is, "What if it's my boss who constantly invites me to meetings or interrupts me?"

We certainly recognize the tension this can create. You want to be an *all in* team member, but you also don't want to be a few weeks away from turning in your two-week notice while ugly crying.

If your team leader is the one constantly pulling you aside, start by being a good improv partner, as we discussed in Chapter 2 (Optimism)—ask your team leader for her advice. Below are a few examples.

"Yes, I'd be happy to help. I had timeboxed this hour to work on the report you needed; would you like me to change my plans, or can I start this at 11 a.m.?"

"Yes, I'd be happy to jump in this meeting with you. I was working on that follow-up email we discussed earlier—would you like me to finalize that, or is this meeting my new priority?"

"I'd be happy to put this on my to-do list. Tomorrow I was planning to gather those numbers you requested. Should I do this project first or go ahead and gather those numbers and then get to this?"

This response works well because it's clear and assertive, without being aggressive. Many times, your team leader gives you multiple projects to work on without even realizing it. They don't do this to be mean; they do this because they have so many plates spinning, and it's difficult to keep track of it all. Kindly reminding them of what's on your to-do list helps you keep your priorities in order.

A good rule of thumb we've found helpful is this: if you feel like you have multiple top priorities, seek clarification. Why? Priorities are always force ranked. A "priority" is a fact or condition that is regarded as more important than another. Priorities can change, but they are always force ranked. It's impossible to have multiple first priorities.

To build attention endurance, you must train. You must give yourself time during the day to tune out distractions and focus.

IDEA #2: BE SMART ABOUT TIMING

Author Daniel Pink published a book in 2018 called *When: The Scientific Secrets of Perfect Timing*. This book introduced us to a concentration- and patience-building life hack.

The basic idea is this: Everyone's day can be broken into three parts. A peak, a trough, and a rebound. Your mood rises in the morning, dips in the afternoon, and rises again in the evening.

Practically speaking, as your mood rises in the morning, this is when your energy levels and brain functioning are at their best. During your peak, you find it easier to concentrate, easier to ignore distractions, and easier to do deep work.

As your mood begins to decline, your energy levels and brain function are on the decline. During the trough, everything that was easier during the peak is suddenly more of a challenge.

In the evening, your energy levels begin to return, and the ability to concentrate and accomplish deep work returns.

This peak, trough, rebound cycle seems to happen every day. The times might vary based on when you wake up each day, but the pattern remains the same. Your brain is at its best during the first four hours after you wake up, hits a mid-day lull, and then rebounds mid-afternoon.

Each time we share this research with other aspiring leaders, they nod their heads in agreement. Chances are high you've experienced this rhythm. You are not the only person who struggles to concentrate shortly after lunch. You are not the only person who feels like taking a nap at 2:55 p.m. each day (which, by the way, according to one British survey is the *worst* minute of the day for everyone).[56]

Here's the point: Sometimes, improving your patience and concentration doesn't involve willpower and discipline. Sometimes improving your patience and concentration involves thinking differently about your day.

Simply being more thoughtful about *when* you try to accomplish certain tasks can make a huge improvement in your ability to concentrate and build patience. Blocking out your mornings for the work that requires your best effort and creativity can pay serious dividends. Pushing back your mundane tasks to the trough hours is a great way to ensure your brain is at its best when you need it at its best.

---

56   Justin Caba, "Least Productive Time of the Day Officially Determined to be 2:55 p.m.: What Can You Do to Stay Awake?," *Medical Daily*, June 4, 2013, https://www.medicaldaily.com/least-productive-time-day-officially-determined-be-255-pm-what-you-can-do-stay-awake-246495.

IDEA #3: STAY FOCUSED ON WHAT YOU CAN CONTROL

Shortly after Al Gore's book *An Inconvenient Truth* was released in 2006, climate change became a much larger part of the national conversation. As a result, a pithy phrase that originated in the 1970s suddenly became very popular. That phrase is, "Think global, act local."

As far as pithy phrases go, this one is pretty stellar. Four words; two contrasting verbs, and two contrasting nouns. That's not easy to do.

We share this because we believe there is a lot of wisdom in these four words. Not just for the environment, but also for your ability to develop patience.

The beauty of "think global, act local" is that it takes a *massive* idea (caring for our planet) and distills it down to something attainable and actionable (do small things around your house to make a difference). We like to call this *differentiating between desires and goals.* Let's explain because we think this is a big deal.

One of the main reasons people get distracted from important projects is they confuse desires and goals.[57] What's the difference? Glad you asked.

A desire is anything in life that you want, but which you and you alone cannot control. A goal, on the other hand, is anything in life you want, but which you and you alone do control.

Let's keep using the example about the planet.

---

57   Thank you to our friend, Dr. Randy Marshall, for introducing us to this concept.

You want to help care for the planet. The question you need to ask is, "Do you and you alone have control to achieve what you want?" The answer, of course, is no. There are almost eight billion other people on this planet and countless organizations, and you cannot make those people or those organizations do anything. You have no control over them and their behaviors.

You *want* to take care of the planet, but you and you alone cannot achieve what you want. That means caring for the planet is a *desire*.

However, don't give up! This doesn't mean all is lost. You can still set *goals* that you believe will make a difference in helping you achieve your *desire*. Watch.

You don't control the other eight billion people on the planet, but what do you control? What can you and you alone begin to do? What are actions you can take that are not dependent on anyone else? What are some things you can put on your to-do list that are dependent on you and you alone? When you ask the questions that way, you begin to see some clear answers. These clear answers are your *goals*.

You can recycle. You can use cloth napkins rather than paper napkins. You can buy an electric vehicle. You can switch to LED light bulbs. You can make donations to organizations that are fighting climate change. You can purchase fewer items. The list goes on and on.

Even though taking care of the planet is not dependent upon you and you alone, that doesn't mean you should give up and not try. The key to long-term engagement in these efforts is to be super clear about what's a win for you. It means you need to be crystal clear on what's a desire and what's a goal. If you keep believing it's your job to save the planet, then you'll quickly get discouraged and possibly quit.

Desires are the results of activities. They are unscheduled and unpredictable. We need to hold loosely to our desires.

Goals are related to activities under our control. They are scheduled and predictable. We need to hold tightly to our goals.

This distinction between desires and goals has huge implications on your professional life. If you were to ask people at the beginning of the year to discuss their professional goals, you'd quickly hear that their list is filled with desires, not goals. Their list is filled with things they want, but which they and they alone do not control.

My goal is to get promoted.

My goal is to grow sales by 15 percent.

My goal is to pass the CPA exam.

All of those items are great things to want, but they are not things you and you alone control. The last we checked, bosses determine who gets promoted; customers choose how to spend their money; and when it comes to the CPA exam, you have no clue if the questions will match what you've studied.

The way to take your desires and turn them into goals—things which you and you alone can control—is as follows:

DESIRE	GOAL
My desire is to get promoted.	*My goal is to read four leadership books and volunteer for two new projects.*
My desire is to grow sales by 15 percent.	*My goal is to contact fifteen potential prospects each week.*
My desire is to pass the CPA exam.	*My goal is to study sixty minutes a day, five days a week.*

Now, you might be thinking to yourself, *I get it, but this just sounds like semantics. What does it matter?* This matters a lot. As we said above, this is the key to long-term, patient engagement in things that matter.

Keeping things focused on what you and you alone can control doesn't promote selfishness; it promotes endurance. It keeps you motivated. It keeps you energized.

If you want to focus on something for a long period of time, you must have the ability to stay laser-focused on what you can control. That is the key to patient endurance. I have seen so many people give up on doing important things because they are trying to control something they can't, and they get frustrated when they don't achieve it.

The ability to differentiate between what you can and cannot control is not just a key to professional endurance—it's a key to happiness. It's a key to being able to evaluate your career and your personal development. It's a key to sleeping well at night, knowing you are not a victim all day, every day to the whims and desires of other people. When you begin to separate life into the things you do control and don't control, you achieve clarity. Clarity, as we've said a few times, inspires action.

BEHIND ALL GREATNESS IS LONELY DISCIPLINE

Timeboxing (Idea #1) the right moments (Idea #2) to work on the right things (Idea #3) is the key to developing patience and mental endurance.

We'll leave you with one final thought: *behind all greatness is lonely and patient discipline.*

Think about your favorites in life—musicians, artists, athletes, actors, authors, leaders. While most people are watching TikTok videos or shopping on Amazon, your favorites in life were most likely doing something productive. We'll go one step further: they were most likely doing something productive while *no one* was watching. Let's go another step further: they were doing something productive while no one was watching, and without someone telling them what to do.

The secret to greatness isn't a secret at all. It's patience and discipline. Chances are, you already know this.

Greatness is out there for anyone who *wants* it and is willing to put down their phone, turn off the TV, and quit sleeping through their alarm. As we said in the introduction, the bar is low. Your friends and peers are wasting their lives on excessive pleasure. Greatness is there for the taking—if you want it.

One of the most important skills needed today is the ability to manage your attention and say no to the siren call of pleasure and distraction that is around you 24/7. As Stanford neuroscientist Andrew Huberman says, "Those who will be successful, young or old, are going to be those people who can create their own internal buffers. They are going to be able to control their relationship with pleasures because the proximity to pleasures and their availability is the problem."[58]

If you want to make a mark on this world, if you want to stand out, if you want to develop an EDGE and take control of your career, then you need to learn how to manage your attention and develop patient endurance. Two minutes of "boredom while brushing your teeth" over an extended period of time will ultimately lead to a lifetime of accomplishment that you'll be proud to look back on.

Does anyone balance patience and discipline with pleasure and self-indulgence perfectly? Certainly not anyone we know. But the people who consistently show up, work hard, lean into conflict, and sacrifice pleasure for a little more discipline and productivity are the ones we see steadily making progress in their careers and personal lives. Is it glamorous? Not really. Is it guaranteed to deliver a meteoric rise to the top? Probably not. The time-tested path is filled with many moments of steady, lonely, and patient discipline.

58 Andrew Huberman, "Neuroscientist: 'First Hour of the Morning is CRUCIAL,'" Be Inspired, October 6, 2021, YouTube video, https://www.youtube.com/watch?v=jBwM-mCLQQo.

CONCLUSION

THE REMINDER: YOUR REPUTATION SHOWS UP FIRST

As we mentioned at the beginning of this book, most team leaders are looking for the exact same thing as the Clemson football coaching staff. Most team leaders want more than talent. They want the combination of talent *and* attitude.

We've done our best to outline the simplest and easiest way to stand out by showing you're *all in*. As a bonus for finishing the book, here is a cheat sheet (you can find a copy of this at MyEDGEBook.com):

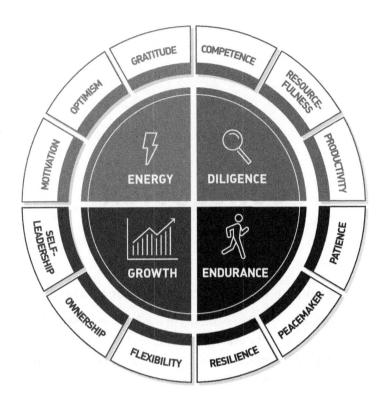

Energy, Diligence, Growth, and Endurance will give your career an EDGE.

Remember, ambition always attracts attention. Emotional commitment gives you an advantage over your peers. Why does this matter? Because for the first ten to fifteen years of your career, decisions about your career's trajectory will be made in rooms where you are not physically present. This is one of the unfortunate realities of your career.

The more ambition and commitment you show, the stronger your reputation grows. It's your reputation that makes it into that room where decisions are made. Before you step into the room, your name has been mentioned in the room. Before you're present in the room, your impact is known in the room—reputation before presence.

THE FIVE SIMPLE NEXT STEPS

Now you know what it takes to develop a favorable reputation. So in addition to practicing the principles and skills discussed in this book, what should you do now?

1. **Schedule a meeting with your team leader.** Ask them which of these strategies they believe you need to work on the most. Start there. As an emerging leader, your team leader is someone you need to know and understand. For now, their opinion matters.

2. **Take a deep breath.** You can't work on all these strategies at the same time. So don't freak out. Keep this book handy and remind yourself often of the type of professional you are trying to become.

3. **Teach this to others.** As you progress in your career, you will get the opportunity to develop others. Using these strategies is a great coaching guide. The more you teach and share these principles with others, the better you will understand them.

4. **Define your success the right way.** This might be the most important thing we say in this book. If you follow these strategies, you will become a different kind of person. In the end, *that's more important than a job title.* If you don't end up where you dreamed you'd be, but you end up making wherever you are better, you've won. That's "success." Be proud.

5. Visit **MyEDGEBook.com.** Our website is filled with additional resources and next steps. Everything from one-on-one coaching calls to Zoom meetups to video resources and audio files are available to help you maintain momentum on this journey.

THE WORLD NEEDS YOU

The world has some big problems. We don't need to list them. You already know.

One person can create a huge problem, but that doesn't mean one person can fix a huge problem. The crowning achievement of humanity is not our ability to create problems. That's easy and, candidly, not worth celebrating. The crowning achievement of humanity is our ability to come together as a team and solve big problems. That is not easy. When it happens, it's worth celebrating.

You get to play a part in all of this. The world needs healthy teams, and healthy teams are led by healthy leaders. Be a healthy leader.

Don't make it your goal in life to be a superhero. Make it your purpose in life to lead a super-team. In the end, that will be more satisfying and more fun than trying to become the next superhero—because nothing beats a healthy team.

Lead with excellence and enjoy the ride.

As you close this book, you've got a decision to make.

Do you set this on your shelf and just feel smarter, or do you put these principles into practice?

We can't force you to do anything. You have all the chips. You have the drive, the knowledge, and the abilities to make a difference. We are hoping you go *all in*, gain an EDGE, and stand out.

You have the power. Go make a difference!

ACKNOWLEDGMENTS

ADAM TARNOW

Thank you to Ann Piper, Laura Cail, Eliece Pool, and the rest of the team at Scribe Media. I now understand why authors thank their editors and publishing teams. You all made this final product *so much better*. I'm amazed and grateful for each of you!

To my co-author, David Morrison, you are truly one of the most encouraging and fun people I've ever met. I'm honored to count you as a friend. It has been so much fun to go through this journey with you, and I look forward to many more!

To all the amazing leaders who cared enough to teach me so many of the ideas that found their way onto the pages of this book: Steve Tarnow, Garfield Lindo, Adam Landrum, John Reeves, Bob Strickland, Bill Willits, David Brooks, Collen Harrison, John McGee, Blake Holmes, Robbie Rice, Scott Kedersha, Lane Blair, Tim Jackson, Barry Adamson, Dale Johnston, Jonathan Pokluda, Todd Wagner, Daniel Crawford, Jeff Strese, Randy Marshall, Matt Briggs, and Clay Scroggins. Thank you!

To all the amazing leaders who I've never met personally but took the time to share their ideas with the world via books, TED Talks, and podcasts: Andy Stanley, Louie Giglio, Patrick Lencioni, Daniel Pink, Adam Grant, Jim Collins, Sheryl Sandberg, Kim Scott, David Epstein, and Erica Dhawan, just to name a few. Thank you!

To The Beach Crew (David, Julia, Ava, Abby, Bradley, Annabelle, Chris, Rachel, Campbell, and Call): your friendship and encouragement are a gift. My family is lucky to have friends like you. Thank you!

Finally, to my family: Jake, Joshua, and Jackie. Honestly, there is not a group of people I'd rather go through life with than you three. You bring me inexpressible joy. I love you! Thank you for cheering me on!

DAVID MORRISON

I will start by thanking my wife, Julia. You are the best leader I know. Thank you for always listening, even when it's half-crazy. You've saved all the readers of this book a lot of time by editing me down to what's helpful and allowable for public consumption. You are the voice in my head pushing me to be better. Thank you.

To my kids, Ava, Abby, Bradley, and Annabelle: you make me look better than I am. Thank you.

To my co-author, Adam Tarnow, who told me five years ago I should keep writing. Without your encouragement, I would not be writing. Thanks for being a friend, a coach, and an encouragement.

To my friend Chris Shelton who has always encouraged me to step up and lead. You're an all-around good dude. You make me want to be better, thank you. I'm grateful to call you a friend.

To Mazen Albatarseh, who taught me what servant leadership looks like in real life. You opened the door, and you opened my eyes to all that leadership is and can be. Your coaching is the edge I needed to be successful, and that's the truth. Action changes things, love is accountable, act as if...And the list goes on and on of the leadership lessons I have learned being around you. I am forever in your debt, brother. I'm ever grateful to you for your authenticity, patience, coaching, and friendship.

To my team: Laura Maravi, Jessie Graham, Richard McCracken, Ken Guardino, and Dena Smith. Leading alongside of you is the best job I ever had.

To the Tacala Senior Leadership Team, thank you for trusting me to lead with you. I am grateful for your partnership in business and your friendship in life.

To the Area Coaches, Restaurant Leaders, and Team Members of Tacala, thank you. It is my greatest privilege to lead such a group as you. You daily display kindness, grit, responsibility, and hard work. I have grown up with you. You have taught me so much about work, leadership, partnership, and team. Thank you for being a constant example of what happens when a group of people decide to be "goodr" together.

To all the people who had a hand in my growth as a leader and a person: Robbie Rice, Claire Blacksher, Giji Kurian, Mario Valladares, Javier Maravi, Oscar Arnold, Derrick Kelsey, Ryan Micks, Bart Box, Daphne Parker, Erica Davidson, and Jesus Mieses.

Made in the USA
Coppell, TX
07 June 2023

17827907R00146